LIFTING AS THEY CLIMBED

LIFTING AS THEY CLIMBED

Mapping a History of Trailblazing Black Women in Chicago

Essence McDowell
Mariame Kaba

Haymarket Books
Chicago, Illinois

Published in 2023 by
Haymarket Books
P.O. Box 180165
Chicago, IL 60618
773-583-7884
www.haymarketbooks.org
info@haymarketbooks.org

ISBN: 978-1-64259-901-5

Distributed to the trade in the US through Consortium Book Sales and Distribution
(www.cbsd.com) and internationally through Ingram Publisher Services
International (www.ingramcontent.com).

This book was published with the generous support of Lannan Foundation, Wallace
Action Fund, and the Marguerite Casey Foundation.

Special discounts are available for bulk purchases by organizations and
institutions. Please email info@haymarketbooks.org for more information.

Cover design by Essence McDowell.
Book design by Jamie Kerry.
Location photographs by Sarah Jane Rhee.

Library of Congress Cataloging-in-Publication data is available.

Entered into digital printing July 2023.

CONTENTS

LIST OF WOMEN

ADA SOPHIA DENNISON MCKINLEY: influential social welfare activist; founder, South Side Settlement House, now known as Ada S. McKinley Community Services ▪ ⚒ ♣

ADDIE LORAINE WYATT: leader in the labor movement and civil rights activist; cofounder, Coalition of Labor Union Women ▪ ⚒ ♣ ♣

AGNES LATTIMER: medical leader, pediatrician, and activist; first Black woman named medical director of a major hospital ▪ ⑤ ♣

ALICE CROLLEY BROWNING: editor and writer; founder of the *Negro Story* magazine, cofounder of the International Black Writers Conference ▪ ♥ ✎ ▥

AMANDA JANE BERRY SMITH: major figure in evangelist and temperance movements; built school and home for Black children in 1800s ♣ ⌂ ⚒

ANNABEL CAREY PRESCOTT: award-winning educator, civil rights activist, and human rights researcher ⌂ ◉ ♣ ▥

ANNIE MINERVA TURNBO MALONE: philanthropist and pioneer in the African American beauty industry; founder, Poro College and Poro Headquarters ⚒ ⑤ ♥

BARBARA JONES-HOGU: seminal artist in the Black Arts Movement; lifetime educator and founding member of AfriCOBRA ▪ ◉ ✎

BESSIE COLEMAN: first African American pilot and aerial performer ▪

BOBBIE L. STEELE: political organizer and educator; the longest-serving African American woman in the history of the Cook County government ▪ ♣ ◉

BRENETTA HOWELL BARRETT: influential community organizer and journalist; founder of extensive community organizations and programs ▪ ✎ ▥ ♣ ⚒

CARDISS COLLINS: political leader; the first Black woman to be elected to Congress from the Midwest, and one of the longest-serving women in the history of Congress ▪ ♣

CARRIE E. BULLOCK: nurse and nursing leader for over four decades 💼 🤝

CHARLEMAE HILL ROLLINS: writer and head librarian of the children's department at the Chicago Public Library; influential in shaping African American voices in children's literature 💼 📖 🎓

CLARA MUHAMMAD: educator and community leader; founder, University of Islam and Muslim Girls Training schools 💼 🛠️ 🎓 🤝 ⛪

CLARICE DURHAM: educator, community organizer, and political activist; cofounder, United States Progressive Party of 1948 🗂️ 🎓

CORA CARROLL: business owner and community activist; first woman elected as the Mayor of Bronzeville 🗂️ 💡

DIANE NASH: award-winning civil rights activist, lifetime organizer, and educator 🏙️ 🗂️

EDITH SPURLOCK SAMPSON: lawyer and civil rights activist; the first Black US delegate appointed to the United Nations, and first Black woman judge in Illinois 💼 🗂️

ELIZABETH LINDSAY DAVIS: historian and pioneer in the Black women's club movement; founder, Phyllis Wheatley Home for Girls 🛠️ 📖 👥 🎓

EMMA JANE ATKINSON: community activist and abolitionist who assisted fugitive enslaved from the south 🏠 🗂️

ERA BELL THOMPSON: international journalist, award-winning author, and notable literary figure in the Chicago Black Renaissance movement 📖 ✒️

Role Key

🏠 Black Old Settler	🎓 Educator	✒️ Journalist
💼 Great Migration	👥 Club Woman	💡 Entrepreneur
🏙️ Chicago Native	⛪ Religious Figure	🗂️ Activist/Organizer
🛠️ Institution Builder	💲 Philanthropist	🤝 Community Leader
🖌️ Artist	📖 Writer	

ETHEL LOIS PAYNE: award-winning journalist and international correspondent; first Black women accredited to the White House Press Corps

ETTA MOTEN BARNETT: renowned singer, stage and film actress, community activist, and philanthropist

EUDORA JOHNSON BINGA: businesswoman and real estate owner; cofounder, Binga State Bank, one of the first Black-owned businesses in Chicago

EUNICE WALKER JOHNSON: fashion pioneer; founder, Ebony Fashion Fair and Fashion Fair Cosmetics; cofounder, Johnson Publishing Company

FANNIE BARRIER WILLIAMS: distinguished political organizer, women's rights leader, writer, and cofounder of multiple organizations and institutions

FANNIE HAGEN EMANUEL: community leader and one of the earliest Black women physicians; founder, Emanuel Settlement House

FLORENCE BEATRICE SMITH PRICE: internationally renowned composer and pianist; first Black female composer to have a symphony performed by an American orchestra

FLORINE REYNOLDS IRVING STEPHENS: entrepreneur and owner of a multimillion-dollar policy wheel business

GEORGIANA ROSE SIMPSON: educator and scholar; the first Black woman to receive a PhD from the University of Chicago, and one of the first Black women in the nation to receive a PhD

GERTRUDE SNODGRASS: community leader and organizer; cofounder, Greater Chicago Food Depository

GWENDOLYN BROOKS: author and Illinois poet laureate; first Black writer to be awarded the Pulitzer Prize

HARRIET ALLEYNE RICE: award-winning international physician; first Black woman to graduate from Wellesley College

HELENA WILSON: national organizer; leader in the Brotherhood of Sleeping Car Porters, Colored Women's Economic Council, and International Ladies' Auxiliary

IDA BELL WELLS-BARNETT: famous antilynching activist, journalist, community leader, clubwoman, and institution builder

IDA GRAY NELSON ROLLINS: institution builder and clubwoman; first Black woman to earn a doctor of dental surgery degree

IDA PLATT: first Black woman to earn an Illinois law license, and the third Black woman lawyer in the nation

IRENE MCCOY GAINES: renowned community leader and first Black woman to run for the Illinois state legislature; founder, Chicago Council of Negro Organizations

JOAN FOSTER MCCARTY: Black Panther Party member, community organizer, educator, and theater professional

JOAN GRAY: Black Panther activist, dancer, and arts administrator

JORJA ENGLISH PALMER: community leader and organizer; founder, Stanford English Home for Boys, Illinois's first group home for African American children

JUANITA "ARIZONA" DRANES: gospel music pioneer, pianist, and singer

KATHERINE DUNHAM: trained dancer, social anthropologist, and choreographer; founder, Ballet Nègre, one of the first Black ballet companies in the United States

KOKO TAYLOR: musical icon and famous blues vocalist

LEANITA MCCLAIN: award-winning journalist, commentator, and columnist for Chicago and national publications

LILLIAN "LIL" HARDIN ARMSTRONG: jazz pianist, bandleader, and influential composer

LORRAINE HANSBERRY: award-winning playwright and civil rights activist; first African American woman to have a play on Broadway

LUCINDA "LUCY" MADDEN SMITH: influential religious figure and social service leader; founded the first Chicago church ever established and led by a woman pastor

LUCY ELDINE GONZALEZ PARSONS: leading figure in the labor movement, organizer, radical socialist, and anarchist communist

MADELINE ROBINSON MORGAN STRATTON MORRIS: educator and activist; developed the first Black history curriculum used by a major US city's public school system

MAHALIA JACKSON: legendary gospel singer, performer, and civil rights activist

MAMIE TILL-MOBLEY: civil rights activist and mother of Emmett Till

MARGARET ALLISON BONDS: child prodigy, influential composer, and pianist; first African American featured soloist with the Chicago Symphony Orchestra

MARGARET TAYLOR GOSS BURROUGHS: prominent activist, writer, and poet; founder, DuSable Museum of African American History

MARIAN CAMPFIELD: journalist; city editor, *Chicago Bee*; women's editor, *Chicago Defender*

MARJORIE STEWART JOYNER: inventor of the permanent wave machine, leader in the beauty industry, philanthropist, and civil rights activist

MARVA COLLINS: renowned educator and author; founder, Westside Preparatory School

MARY FITZBUTLER WARING: influential physician, community leader, educator, and health services provider

MARY GREEN EVANS: influential community leader and social service provider; pastor, Cosmopolitan Community Church

MARY JANE RICHARDSON JONES: prominent abolitionist and early suffragist; matriarch of one of Chicago's oldest communities

MAUDELLE TANNER BROWN BOUSFIELD: educator; first Black woman to graduate from the University of Illinois, first Black principal at two Chicago public high schools 💼 🎓 📖

MELISSA ANN ELAM: community activist; founder, Melissa Ann Elam Home for Working Women and Girls 🏠 🛠 🕸

MINNIE RIPERTON: acclaimed singer, songwriter, and women's health advocate 🏢 🖌 🕸

MITTIE MAUDE LENA GORDON: community leader and organizer; founder, Peace Movement of Ethiopia, the largest Black nationalist organization established by a woman in the US 💼 🕸 🤝

NANCY B. JEFFERSON: influential grassroots organizer known as the "mother of the West Side"; led the MidWest Community Council and founded multiple organizations 🕸 🤝

NORA HOLT: international composer, music critic, and founder of multiple music organizations; first Black woman to earn a master's degree in music 💼 🖌

OLIVE MYRL DIGGS: journalist and human relations worker; managing editor, *Chicago Bee* 🖌 📖

RACHEL REBECCA RIDLEY: community organizer and administrator; driving force behind organizational development and block clubs on the West Side 💼 🕸 🛠 🤝

ROBERTA EVELYN WINSTON MARTIN: gospel music icon, pianist, singer, and composer; founder, Roberta Martin Studio of Music 💼 🛠 🖌 📖

SOPHIA BELL BOAZ: lawyer and social worker; one of the first Black women admitted to the National Association of Women Lawyers 💼

THYRA EDWARDS: noted international activist, foreign correspondent, writer, and advocate for women and children 💼 🎓 📖 🖌 🕸

VIOLETTE NEATLEY ANDERSON: lawyer; first Black woman to graduate from law school in Illinois; first Black woman to practice law before the US Supreme Court; first woman to be assistant prosecutor in Chicago 🕸

VIVIAN CARTER: founder, Vee-Jay Records 🛠 💡

VIVIAN GORDON HARSH: librarian and historian; first African American to head a branch of the Chicago Public Library; developed a world-renowned Black history collection 🏠 🏢 🤝 🤲

WILLIE P. CHERRY: clubwoman, civic worker, Sunday school teacher, and member of the historic West Side Cherry family 🖧 🤝

WILLIE TAPLIN BARROW: civil rights leader and community organizer; cofounder, Operation Breadbasket and Rainbow PUSH Coalition 💼 🛠 ⛪ 🤲 🖧

ZELDA "JACKIE" JACKSON ORMES: first female African American cartoonist, editor, and artist 💼 📖 ✏ 🖌

PREFACE TO THE FIRST EDITION

Mariame Kaba

I moved to Chicago from my hometown of New York City in 1995. In 2016–two decades later–I returned to NYC. In the twenty-one years I spent in Chicago, I immersed myself in the city's history. My personal studies and excursions focused on landmarks and locations relevant to the histories of Black people in the Windy City.

In 2012, as part of an exhibition I cocurated titled Black/Inside, I co-organized a guided tour of locations relevant to Black Chicagoans' captivity and criminalization. We visited the house where Fred Hampton was murdered by Chicago police, the former site of George Jackson's home, **Ida Bell Wells-Barnett's home, the Hull-House Museum, Quinn Chapel,** and more. When this tour was well received, I began to conceive another one, this time focused on the histories of Black women's activism in Chicago.

Over the years, I intermittently researched information about Black women who had lived and worked in Chicago from the mid-nineteenth through the mid-twentieth centuries. This led me to read and learn about well-known Black women activists and artists like **Mary Jane Richardson Jones, Lorraine Hansberry, Mahalia Jackson, Ida Bell Wells-Barnett, Gwendolyn Brooks, Irene McCoy Gaines,** and **Addie Loraine Wyatt,** among others. Over time, I discovered lesser-known Chicago Black women like **Charlemae Hill Rollins, Fannie Barrier Williams,** **Sophia Bell Boaz, Mary Green Evans,** and **Emma Jane Atkinson.**

In early 2017, I hit a wall as I struggled to complete this project. I considered abandoning it altogether. When I posted about this on Facebook, several friends and comrades encouraged me to continue with the tour and offered their help to finish it. In October of that same year, I presented the work in progress to a group of Black women friends. One of them, Essence McDowell, was excited enough to lend her skills and time in support of the project.

Essence and I decided that we would begin by publishing a guidebook focused on mapping some of the many activist and artistic contributions to Chicago made by Black women from the city's South Side. The publication you are reading is the culmination of our collaboration. Without Essence's partnership, this guidebook would not exist. My hope is that people of all ages in Chicago and beyond will experience the publication as an introduction to Black women's contributions to building the city. It would please me enormously if Black girls and young women used this book to explore and learn about the legacies of their foremothers. I hope it shapes their ideas about what they can accomplish and inspires in them a desire to travel the city and the world, learning more about their own histories as well as those of others.

Finally, there are many people to thank for making this guidebook possible. I am especially grateful to: Essence McDowell, Sarah Jane Rhee, Rachel Wallis, Nicole Marroquin, Mina Marroquin-Crow, Michael Linus Owens, Rebecca Zorach, Kierra Verdun, Pamela Quintana, Keisha Farmer-Smith, Tanuja Jagernauth, Lori Barcliff Baptista, Mandi Hinkley Wolfman, Buck Doyle, Lillian Cartwright, Natalie Bennett, Dan Cooper, Ashon Crawley, and Mia Henry.

INTRODUCTION

Essence McDowell

In my time teaching and touring *Lifting as They Climbed*, one of the most memorable moments occurred when I spoke to students at a South Side math and science high school. I started the discussion by asking what would become the most important question during my school tours: "Can you share some figures in Black women's history that you've learned about in your classes?" The answers started off slow, but one by one, students raised their hands to share. Michelle Obama. Rosa Parks. Harriet Tubman. Maya Angelou. These were the only names most students had learned. Then, I started the *Lifting as They Climbed* animated presentation I had created for the class.

After my presentation, the energy in the room shifted. The students raised their hands with questions and spoke with an excitement that vibrated between us. They boldly shared their experiences with racism in the classroom, revealing how as early as elementary school, they had tried to speak up to get their teachers to include Black history. I did my best to validate their courage and respond with encouragement.

When the talk was over, some of the young women who were a part of the school's Black student organization stayed behind. They hugged me and let me know that the book meant a lot to them. They wanted to make sure other students got copies, and we talked until they had to leave for their next classes. In my memory, this day is wrapped in gold, cementing that this work was deeper than just a guidebook. It had, in fact, become something bigger than I could have imagined.

Since then, I have visited classrooms across the city of Chicago giving similar talks. No matter which school or which part of the city, the students share the same responses and similar stories, and are always hungry to learn. Each time I walk away, it cracks me wide open. First, there's a burst of energy; I'm motivated and swelling with pride at the brilliance of these youth. But what also sticks with me is a profound sadness. I carry the heartache from their stories of public education's disregard of Black history, and its lack of engagement with Black women's history. I can't help but question what allows this systemic erasure to prevail this far into the twenty-first century.

The young women in these classes remind me so much of my younger self. I would sit in school oscillating between anger and despondency, constantly wondering why Black history was a footnote in "American history." While that was nearly two decades ago, I've made a practice of checking high school history textbooks for signs of improvement. To this day, textbooks, especially those in under-resourced communities, remain nearly identical to the ones I was assigned. Black and brown youth deserve to see themselves reflected in the pages of history. Black history is American history.

The need for these narratives goes beyond younger generations. I've had the opportunity to speak with educators, community leaders, and political figures who've been so excited to take the tours and learn these women's stories. These experiences reinforce that I must share all the power I've gained from researching and learning about the women of *Lifting as They Climbed*, and from the undeniable beauty of walking the streets of the South and West Sides, touching what remains of our communal archive.

The process has not been pure empowerment, inspiration, and joy. There have been moments in the journey when I've doubted the necessity of this project. Then events in the news or challenges within my community shake me out of it, and I remember that I have a blueprint in my hands. We can look to the women of *Lifting as They Climbed* to ground ourselves in another transformative century in history. Most of the women this book features came up through the Great Migration. The growing population was met with a complete lack of infrastructure to support or provide for it. Many of the institutions and organizations these women created were born out of the dire need for social services, including housing, employment, education, and health care. Because the same powerful forces still

shape material realities, these same challenges continue to plague our communities.

If we aim to embody the liberation we dream of, studying Black women's history offers glimpses of a way forward. Their legacies continue to enlighten and uplift me each time I revisit these pages. This guidebook, and the landmarks it includes, have deepened my love for Chicago and redefined my visions of the possibilities for my communities. For these reasons and more, I'm committed to sharing this work with the world for as long as I am able.

The additions were chosen with intention, in hopes that the amplification of these lives reverberate into the present day. Creating the West Side tour was the hardest and most vital undertaking for the extension of the guidebook. With the help of researchers, archivists, and community members, we were able to capture over 150 years of West Side history, from **Harriet Alleyne Rice**, who became a physician in the post-Civil War era; to renowned leader and political activist **Brenetta Howell Barrett**, who has spent over sixty years building community organizations; to **Gertrude Snodgrass**, whose tireless commitment fed thousands facing food insecurity on the West Side. All in all, the new tour gives readers a glimpse into the vast innovation and brilliance that Black women have poured into West Side communities.

What type of world will exist by the time this book reaches your hands?

The answer seems as fragile as it is unknowable. But so much about the history told in this guidebook thrives in the present and informs our answers about the future. There has been no greater gift than dedicating these years to telling these stories; my life has not been the same since Mariame invited me to collaborate on this book project in 2017. It has also been an immeasurable honor to work alongside her over the years and to learn from her. Much like the legacies we unearthed together, she is the living embodiment of what it means to "Lift as You Climb." I am forever grateful for Mariame. Thank you—these years of collaboration and friendship have been absolutely transformative.

I want to give a huge thank-you to researchers Ariel Atkins and Tonia Hill for their invaluable contributions. I have no idea what I would have done without your support, countless hours, and input. I also want to send a big thank-you to Leah Gibson and her SAIC students: Madison Neel, Alicia Morgan, Anna Elise Adami, Nadia Frierson, and Alyson Houdyschell. I'm grateful to the many educators who allowed me to share these histories with their students, and to Jennifer Johnson for her constant kindness and generosity as I navigated the CPS class visits that shifted my whole world. And the deepest, most infinite appreciation to my family and community, who help to keep me sane, laughing, and writing through the most challenging times of our lives. Nicole Stanley, Aja Reynolds, Marco Roc, Sarah Oberholzer, Ebony Kennedy, Lilian Paniagua, and Tiffany Johnson—I am more whole with you all. I also couldn't finish without sending much gratitude to Anne Kosseff-Jones for sharing her thorough and thoughtful editing prowess, and to the brilliant Natalie Bennett who uplifted this work and provided the support of the UIC Women's Leadership and Resource Center.

Most importantly, I give thanks to my ancestors and the women of *Lifting as They Climbed*.

Umuntu ngumuntu ngabantu: I am, because you are.

ABOUT THIS BOOK

Lifting as They Climbed: Mapping a History of Black Women on the South Side was self-published by the authors in 2018. The first edition sold over a thousand copies in the first few weeks of publishing and quickly went into a second printing. The response from both Chicagoans and readers around the nation was overwhelmingly positive. In 2019, the authors signed with Haymarket Books to extend the project. What started out as a guidebook featuring forty-eight women now features seventy-eight, with a new tour specifically dedicated to the history of Chicago's West Side. The women featured in this book used their gifts to build up their communities. Many did so through leadership in civic, social, and religious organizations pursuing a broad range of projects. Others were artists—writers, painters, musicians, dancers, and others—who both documented the conditions of Black people and shaped culture in Chicago and nationwide. And some were Black women activists who organized to make the city work better for themselves and for their loved ones and communities. Their work was not limited to addressing concerns within the Black community.

We relied on a range of sources—including articles, websites, books, and oral histories—to create both the original guidebook and the new material in this extended version. We looked for evidence of Black women's contributions to Chicago from the mid-nineteenth through the mid-twentieth centuries in particular and are now sharing the fruits of our research. But we know that ours is not an exhaustive account. This story has many limitations, as it focuses on the most visible and identifiable women in our existing archives. Hundreds of thousands of Chicago Black women participated in the movements that we discuss in this book. However, most of their names are lost to history.

We faced challenges documenting Black women's lives and contributions on the West Side of Chicago, despite substantial information-gathering and the support of multiple researchers, scholars, and archivists. (See **West Side introduction** on page 119). We know that there are many more stories to be researched and told. We hope this publication plays a role in encouraging people to seek out other names and to publish their stories, or perhaps even to develop community archives documenting the rich Black history on the West Side.

There are sixty-seven locations divided into five lengthy tours featured in this guidebook. The locations are focused on the South Side, but they extend to Downtown and go into the West Side. These tours are suggestions; we want readers to feel free to create their own tours based on personal interests and travel capacity. While we offer a few configurations, the possibilities are truly endless.

There are some selected mini tours in the back of the guidebook for those who prefer specialized exploration. There's a tour that features activists and a tour for artists and educators who would like to chart the history of Chicago arts and music.

The first edition of this guidebook has been used for educational workshops, organizational tours, conference activities, classroom presentations, college field trips, bike tours, family outings, and so much more. Our desire is that this text continues to be used to explore Chicago in all its magnificence and complexity, so feel free to mark it up and share it with others. We hope that your guidebook will be well worn from frequent use, and that it will pique your interest in digging deeper into Chicago's history.

This is a guidebook, so the descriptions presented are brief and readable for on-the-go use. For those who want to learn more about the people featured in the guide, we list resources for further research at the end of the publication. The website www.LiftingAsTheyClimbed.com also offers more supplementary materials, including curriculum sources, maps, and coloring pages for young people. We are updating our online hub for this expanded edition, so be sure to visit. In addition, we want to hear from readers about your explorations and adventures. Let us know what you think about the book. And finally, we encourage you to share your ideas, research, and leads with us through the website. If you have new names, locations, and landmarks relevant to the histories of Black women in Chicago—especially on the West Side—we would love to know about them.

Our hope is that these stories spread from the neighborhoods of Chicago to around the world. We are so honored to have been able to bring folks along with us on this journey of exploration. May the excavation of Black women's histories, in Chicago and around the nation, continue well beyond these pages.

SOUTH SIDE

Tour 2: Sites of Institutional Impact and Communal Power

Tour 3: The Gateways of Arts and Activism

Tour 4: The Path of Pioneers and Change Agents

UNDERSTANDING SOUTH SIDE HISTORY

When **Emma Jane Atkinson** arrived in Chicago with her husband Isaac in 1847, there were about two hundred other Black people living in the city. By 1850, the Black community in Chicago numbered 323 out of a population of over twenty-three thousand people. During this period, Black people in Illinois could not vote, serve on juries and militias, or testify against white people. In 1870, 3,700 Black people lived in Chicago; by 1880, that number had increased to 6,480, or a little over 1 percent of the city's total population.

Atkinson, **Mary Jane Richardson Jones**, and several other women discussed in this publication were among what Marcia Chatelain termed Chicago's "old settler" community. Chatelain writes: "Old-settler women formed social clubs, mutual aid societies, and churches based on their shared heritage and status as the Black elite of the Midwest." Late nineteenth- and early twentieth-century middle-class Black clubwomen in Chicago had varied interests and took up different causes, including literacy, child welfare, voting rights, and antilynching campaigns. In their club work, these Black women had to focus on both gender issues and racial equality, often in the face of hostility from white women as well as Black and white men.

While there did exist a small Black elite in Chicago, most Black residents were working class or poor. During the late nineteenth and early twentieth centuries, the majority of working Black women in Chicago were servants in white people's homes, office buildings, and hotels. Cynthia Blair explains that in 1890, "77 percent of working Black women in Chicago held jobs as service workers, and 16 percent worked as semiskilled laborers." A subset of women also worked in the sex trade and underground economies. Even though their experiences are more difficult to access because of limited information, we touch upon them, too, in this book.

The composition of Chicago's Black population dramatically changed between 1915 and 1970, when nearly seven million Black people moved from the US South to cities in the Northeast, Midwest, and West. This is an era commonly referred to as the Great Migration. Many migrants who left their homes in the South settled in Chicago to pursue better opportunities in education, employment, and other areas, as well as to escape racial terrorism. Many of the Black women featured in this publication arrived in Chicago during the First Migration, between 1910 and 1940. A few others came to the city during the second wave of the Great Migration, from 1940 to 1970.

During the First Migration, Black Chicago's population increased fivefold from 44,000 in 1910 to 234,000 in 1930. By 1920, 83 percent of Black Chicagoans were born outside of Illinois, with 65 percent of that group coming from the South, according to historian Allen Spear. The newcomers to the city established institutions, including churches, settlement houses, businesses, civic associations, and social clubs. Most lived in the "Black Belt" on the South Side of Chicago. The term "Black Belt" was developed "by sociologists and vice commissions to highlight increased rates of delinquency, dependency, and crime" (Schroeder Schlabach). Historian Davarian L. Baldwin describes it as "a narrow strip of land on the south side of the city from 18th Street to 39th Street and bounded by State Street on the east and the Rock Island Railroad tracks and LaSalle Street on the west".

The commercial, political, and cultural center of the Black Belt was Bronzeville. A positive name coined by *The Chicago Bee* newspaper in the 1930s, it described the skin tone of the community's inhabitants. Over the years, there have been several boundary designations for Bronzeville, which was also known as the Black Metropolis. It initially stretched from 31st to 39th Streets and from State Street to Cottage Grove Avenue. Bronzeville's current boundaries are 26th Street to the north, 51st Street to the south, Cottage Grove Avenue to the east, and the Dan Ryan Expressway to the west. Many of the women featured in this section lived, worked, and

socialized in Bronzeville.

Bronzeville was also the heart of the Chicago Black Renaissance movement from 1930 through the 1950s. Not as well-known as its predecessor, the Harlem Renaissance, the Chicago Black Renaissance was a multidisciplinary arts and cultural movement infused with a Pan-Africanist and internationalist focus on social justice. Many of the artists associated with the Chicago Black Renaissance movement were women and are featured in this guidebook. They include **Gwendolyn Brooks, Margaret Taylor Goss Burroughs, Lorraine Hansberry, Mahalia Jackson, Katherine Dunham, Charlemae Hill Rollins, Thyra Edwards,** and **Alice Crolley Browning.** A set of important institutions was also formed during this period to cultivate the arts, promote a Pan-African identity, and teach children about their ancestors' accomplishments. Some of these institutions still exist today on the South Side, including the **George Cleveland Hall Branch of the Chicago Public Library** and the **South Side Community Art Center** (SSCAC)— which Anne Meis Knupfer describes as "the first Black art museum in the United States."

Alongside this cultural revival, segregation and discrimination took their toll on Black Chicagoans. Rents in the Black Belt were higher than in surrounding white neighborhoods, and housing was substandard. Landlords divided already cramped apartments into kitchenettes and jacked up prices. Far from finding a land of milk

and honey in Chicago, southern migrants often struggled with poverty,
discrimination, and racial terror im-
posed by police and white neighbors.
Despite these struggles, Black people
in Chicago, including the women we
describe in this guidebook, took pride
in their communities, and worked re-
lentlessly to improve them.

The four tours within this section
chronicle the lives of Black women
who have shaped the city's history,
primarily focusing on sites on the
South Side. However, in this new edition, we stretch out the boundaries as
far north as the Chicago Loop area to
include the stories of women like **Eunice Walker Johnson**, the cofounder
of the **Johnson Publishing** empire,
and as far south as the Pullman neighborhood to speak to the legacy of **Helena Wilson** and the labor movement
of the Pullman porters. Drawing from
the many more stories there are to tell,
we add profiles of **Elizabeth Lindsay
Davis** and **Mary Fitzbutler Waring**,
clubwomen who developed housing
and community safe havens. Many
of the problems that these community builders were struggling against
over one hundred years ago continue
to trouble Chicago. We hope that the
more encompassing narratives that
we've included spark interest in how
the past has shaped and currently informs our present. While many of the
issues these women faced persist,
may their stories serve as inspiration
for the solutions.

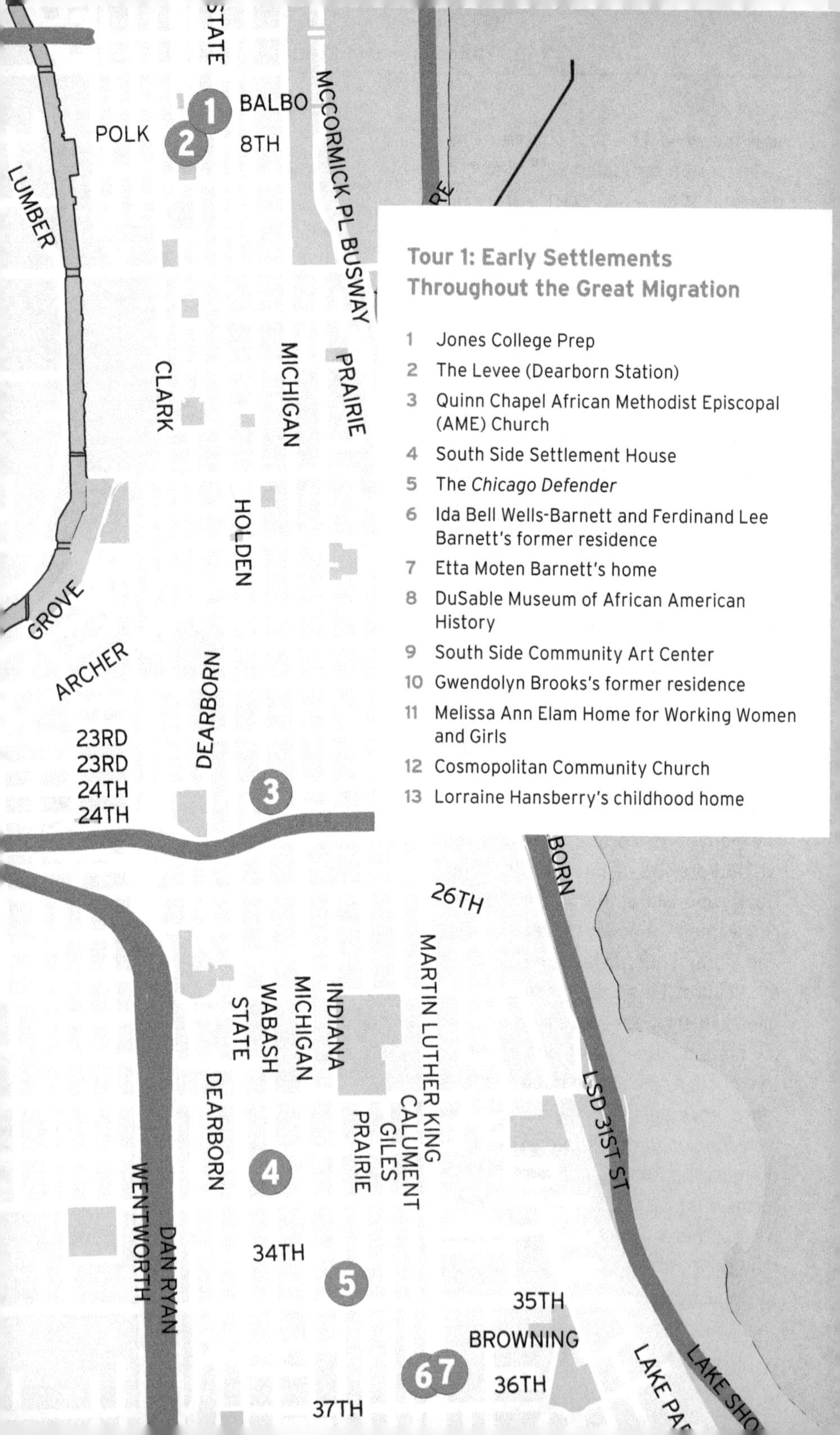

STATE

BALBO

POLK

8TH

MCCORMICK PL BUSWAY

LUMBER

CLARK

MICHIGAN

PRAIRIE

HOLDEN

GROVE

ARCHER

DEARBORN

23RD
23RD
24TH
24TH

**Tour 1: Early Settlements
Throughout the Great Migration**

26TH

BORN

MARTIN LUTHER KING

INDIANA

MICHIGAN

WABASH

STATE

DEARBORN

CALUMENT

GILES

PRAIRIE

WENTWORTH

DAN RYAN

LSD 31ST ST

34TH

35TH

BROWNING

36TH

37TH

LAKE SHO

LAKE PA

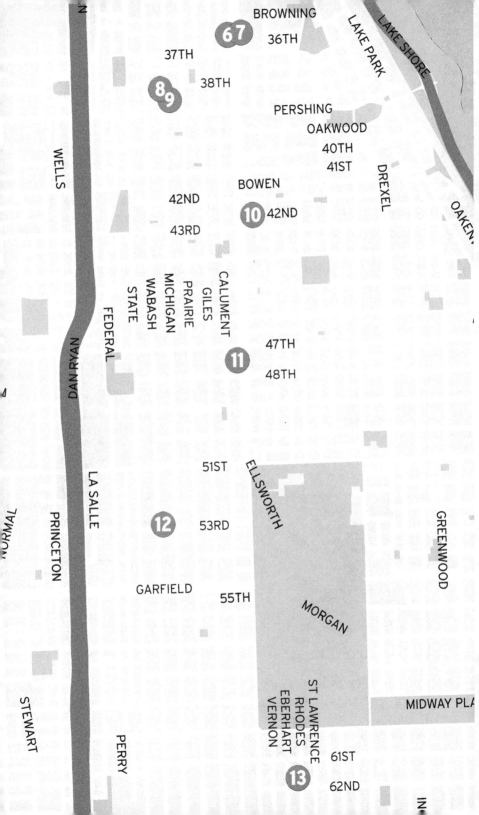

TOUR 1: EARLY SETTLEMENTS THROUGHOUT THE GREAT MIGRATION

This tour gives readers a glimpse into over two hundred years of Black women's history in Chicago, from one of the early Black settlers, abolitionist Mary Jane Richardson Jones; to Melissa Ann Elam and Ada Sophia Dennison McKinley, who built institutions to support and provide for the needs of those migrating into the South Side; to redlining and the housing crisis as illuminated through the story of playwright Lorraine Hansberry's childhood home. Through the sites in this tour, you'll discover parts of the South Side's origin story and the women who were pivotal to its developing neighborhoods during the Great Migration. As readers journey from the Loop to the Black Belt, they are guided to deepen their understanding of the cultural and geographical history of Chicago.

JONES COLLEGE PREP
700 S. State Street

MARY JANE RICHARDSON JONES

October 28, 1819-January 2, 1910
Occupation: abolitionist, suffragist, clubwoman, philanthropist

Mary Jane Richardson Jones was born a free Black woman in Memphis, Tennessee, in 1819; she moved with her family to Alton, Illinois, in 1836. In 1844, she married John Jones, the son of a freed slave whom she had known in Memphis. Together, they moved to Chicago in 1845 with only $3.50 in hand. They joined a very small community—at the time, there were 140 Black people in Chicago.

Mary and John Jones were

abolitionists who played important roles in Chicago's Underground Railroad. Their home and John's tailor shop were both stops on the Railroad, offering refuge to many fugitive slaves who were traveling from the South to cities in the North and in Canada; the couple provided fugitives with clothing, food, and money for transportation. The two were friends with Frederick Douglass, John Brown, and other prominent abolitionists.

The Joneses' home also served as a meeting place for those involved in the fight for women's rights. Susan B. Anthony, Carrie Chatman Catt, and other early feminists met in the Joneses' home. Mary Jones was a major advocate of women's right to vote.

John Jones made a small fortune as a custom tailor with a shop at 119 S. Dearborn Street that catered to rich white men. With Mary's support, John was able to pursue politics and his other interests. In 1871, he became the first Black person to hold elected office in Illinois, serving two terms as Cook County Commissioner. He died in 1879. In his will, John donated land on the corner of Harrison Street and Plymouth Court to the city, with the stipulation that it be used to build a public school. Today, it is part of the site where **Jones College Prep** is located.

Mary Jones lived many more years after her husband's death and was the matriarch of the Black "old settler" community in Chicago. When **Ida Bell Wells-Barnett** founded the first Chicago Black women's club in 1893, she reached out to Jones to "head the movement" as an honorary chair of the club. Founded as the Tourgée Ladies' Club, it was later renamed the Ida B. Wells Club.

Jones died at the age of ninety-one and is buried beside her husband at Graceland Cemetery. Her grave is marked "Grandma Jonesie."

Institutional affiliations

Olivet Baptist Church

Provident Hospital

Tourgée Ladies' Club
(later Ida B. Wells Club)

Phyllis Wheatley Women's Club

Phyllis Wheatley Home for Girls

Quinn Chapel

Additional landmarks and locations

Mary Richardson Jones Park is located at 1240 S. Plymouth Court.

Mary and John Jones lived at 218 Third Avenue and then 43 Ray Street.

116 Edinah Street (now known as Plymouth Court–Ninth Street and Plymouth Court) is the site of the Joneses' last home.

119 S. Dearborn Street is the site of John Jones's tailor shop.

THE LEVEE
(DEARBORN STATION)
47 W. Polk Street

Dearborn Station (also referred to as Polk Street Station) was the oldest of the six intercity train stations serving downtown Chicago. During the height of passenger rail travel in the early 1920s, Dearborn Station hosted 146 trains that carried more than seventeen thousand passengers each day. When the station opened in 1885, it was located at the north end of Chicago's red-light and vice district. Today, the old train station has been converted to retail and office space.

In the late nineteenth and early twentieth centuries, the vice district was called "the Levee." The Levee stretched from Van Buren Street or Harrison Street on the north to 22nd Street on the south, and from Michigan Avenue or Dearborn Street on the east to Clark Street or the Chicago River on the west. It encompassed almost a full square mile of the city's South Side. In her book *Along the Streets of Bronzeville* (2013), Elizabeth Schroeder Schlabach describes the Levee as follows:

> The Levee red-light district made up twenty square blocks; this vice district comprised 500 saloons, six variety theaters, 1,000 "concert halls," fifteen gambling houses, fifty-six pool rooms, and 500 bordellos housing 3,000 female workers. The showplace of the Levee had been the internationally famous Everleigh Club at 2131–2133 Dearborn Street.... Three African American brothels featuring "Colored Gay Ladies of the Night" made themselves available to free-spending Caucasian customers. Several madams of color maintained lucrative establishments and expected healthy profits from the 1893 World's Fair.

The Levee was officially shut down in 1912 by Mayor Carter Harrison.

Racial discrimination limited opportunities for Black migrants to Chicago during the late nineteenth and early twentieth centuries. Some Black women worked in the informal labor market or underground economy as a strategy for dealing with racial segregation and poverty. Examples of informal labor participation include policy or gambling ventures, unlicensed home beauty shops, selling food on the street without a license, babysitting, and sex work. For some of these Black women, mostly those between the ages of nineteen and twenty-seven, sex work was a way to make the money they needed to survive. Most of those women worked in brothels. Black women like Mollie Vinefield, Maggie Douglass, Hattie Johnson, and Vina Fields owned their own brothels and were able to gain some semblance of financial independence. However, they were the exceptions, not the rule.

In her book *I've Got to Make My Livin': Black Women's Sex Work in Turn-of-the-Century Chicago* (2010), historian Cynthia M. Blair provides the following numerical snapshot of sex workers in the Levee:

> In 1880, when African Americans composed 1 percent of the city's population, black women accounted for 15 percent of the 207 Levee prostitutes enumerated by federal census takers. Nineteen percent were white women of foreign birth, and the majority, 66 percent, were native-born white women. Twenty years later, when black women accounted for 2 percent of the city's population and 3 percent of all "gainfully" employed women, their representation among Levee prostitutes remained high. They made up 17 percent of 287 sex workers, while foreign-born white women accounted for 25 percent and native-born white women accounted for 57 percent of the total.

Because they could not afford to pay for protection, Black brothel owners were subjected to constant and consistent police harassment, and their establishments were regularly raided.

More to read

I've Got to Make My Livin': Black Women's Sex Work in Turn-of-the-Century Chicago by Cynthia M. Blair (The University of Chicago Press, 2010)

Along the Streets of Bronzeville: Black Chicago's Literary Landscape by Elizabeth Schroeder Schlabach (University of Illinois Press, 2013)

QUINN CHAPEL AFRICAN METHODIST EPISCOPAL (AME) CHURCH | 2401 S. Wabash Avenue

Quinn Chapel is the oldest Black congregation in Chicago, and perhaps the most important because of the role it has played in the fight for civil and human rights. The chapel started in 1844 as a prayer group of seven people. In 1847, the congregation was officially admitted to the African Methodist Episcopal (AME) Church and moved to the site of what is now the Monadnock Building, located at 53 W. Jackson Boulevard. Quinn Chapel served as a station on the Underground Railroad, and Chicago's abolitionist movement was centered in the church.

The original chapel was destroyed in the Great Chicago Fire in 1871. The church has stood at its present location since 1891. When it was rebuilt, the church was designed by a Black architect and built from the ground up.

Abolitionists John and **Mary Jane Richardson Jones** were members of Quinn Chapel. In 1893, Frederick Douglass addressed an audience of fifteen hundred people at the church on the significance of Haiti, a predominantly Black nation that had gained its independence through a slave revolt.

Quinn Chapel led the fight for and raised much of the money to build **Provident Hospital**, the first Black hospital in the country. Dr. Martin Luther King Jr., Susan B. Anthony, and W. E. B. Du Bois were just a few of the figures who spread their messages from the Quinn Chapel pulpit.

AMANDA JANE BERRY SMITH 🏠 ⚒ ⛪

January 23, 1837-February 25, 1915
Occupation: evangelist, missionary, institution builder, youth services provider

Amanda Jane Berry Smith was a major figure in the evangelist and temperance movements. She went on an international speaking tour in Europe and worked as a missionary in Africa. Berry Smith also built a home and school for Black children—at the time, it was the only institution in Chicago that accepted them. Her funeral was held at **Quinn Chapel** and attended by thousands.

EMMA JANE ATKINSON 🏠 ⛪

Lifespan Dates: Unknown
Occupation: abolitionist, philanthropist, community activist

Chicago abolitionist Emma Jane Atkinson came to Chicago in 1847 with her husband Isaac Atkinson. Scholars believe that Emma was half Black and half Cherokee. Her husband Isaac was the son of Richard Atkinson, born in Scotland, and Cecelia (last name unknown), a member of the Cherokee Nation. Isaac Atkinson owned his own bus line in Chicago before the advent of streetcars.

The Atkinsons lived in Chicago at a time when there were only about two hundred other Black people in the city. By 1850, Black people in Chicago only numbered 378 out of a population of over 23,000 people. The Atkinsons are said to have been the thirteenth Black family to settle in Chicago and were among the city's "old settlers."

Emma Atkinson was one of the mysterious "Big Four," a group of Black women at **Quinn Chapel** who provided food, clothing, and shelter to runaway slaves. Atkinson is currently the only named member of the group—unfortunately, Black abolitionists in Chicago (and elsewhere) who assisted fugitive slaves did not keep written records and accounts of their efforts. As a result, we know almost nothing about the work of the Big Four.

SOUTH SIDE SETTLEMENT HOUSE
3201 S. Wabash Avenue

ADA SOPHIA DENNISON MCKINLEY

June 26, 1868–August 25, 1952
Occupation: organizer, social services
activist, settlement house founder, educator,
community leader

Ada Sophia Dennison McKinley is considered one of the most influential social welfare activists in Chicago's history. She traveled to Chicago from her hometown of Galveston, Texas, toward the end of World War I. In 1919, she started a settlement house providing food resources, relocation assistance, and employment support services for Black soldiers returning from the war and migrants coming in from Southern states. Given the scarcity of public resources, McKinley quickly became a pivotal source for community betterment in Chicago's predominantly Black South Side communities.

With very little financial backing or assistance, McKinley expanded her vision and established South Side Community Services, an organization that would later become the **South Side Settlement House**. Its programs included youth education, foster care and adoption services, recreation activities, and disability support. Many of the services were multigenerational and served a wide demographic, as McKinley sought to reach residents of

Chicago housing projects in the most impoverished neighborhoods.

McKinley addressed the growing needs of the community by incorporating health care services, resources for mothers, and space to produce local publications. Aware of the importance of political organizing, she started a neighborhood civic club and opened the doors for organizations to host meetings and other collective gatherings.

To honor the legacy of McKinley, the **South Side Settlement House** was renamed Ada. S. McKinley Community Services. Almost one hundred years since its inception, Ada S. McKinley Community Services has locations throughout Chicago and is one of the nation's largest institutions providing social services to Black people.

Institutional affiliations

War Camp Community Service
Chicago Commission on Race Relations
Social Workers Round Table
Phyllis Wheatley Club
League of Women Voters of Chicago
Illinois Federation of Republican Colored Women's Clubs

Additional landmarks and locations

Oak Woods Cemetery, 67th Street and Cottage Grove Avenue

THE *CHICAGO DEFENDER* | 3435 S. Indiana Avenue

The *Chicago Defender* newspaper was founded by Robert Sengstacke Abbott in 1905, with a twenty-five cent investment and a few hundred copies of the publication. Originally printed at 3435 S. Indiana Avenue, it was the second Black newspaper in Chicago. The *Defender* contributed to the Great Migration by printing advertisements touting the economic and social opportunities in Chicago, which encouraged Black people to move from Southern states to the North. By World War I, the *Defender* was the largest-selling and most widely distributed Black-owned newspaper in the United States, with two-thirds of its circulation outside of Chicago.

During the civil rights movement of the 1950s and '60s, the *Defender* moved to a building at 2400 S. Michigan Avenue. It increased its circulation by becoming one of the main publications chronicling the events and providing analysis of the movement. The *Defender* has since relocated and is now electronically published at 4445 S. King Drive.

More to read

The Defender: How the Legendary Black Newspaper Changed America by Ethan Michaeli (Houghton Mifflin Harcourt, 2016)

ETHEL LOIS PAYNE
August 14, 1911–May 28, 1991
Occupation: journalist, international correspondent, writer

Ethel Lois Payne was an award-winning journalist heralded as the "first lady of the Black press." Born in Chicago, Payne got her start in journalism in 1951, when she was hired as a reporter for the *Chicago Defender,* where she would work for over twenty years. As a correspondent and columnist for the *Defender* and other outlets, Payne covered politics, civil rights, and international affairs for three decades. Her reporting from thirty countries included interviews with Haile Selassie, Idi Amin, and Zhou Enlai.

Early in her career, Payne became one of the first Black women accredited to the White House Press Corps. She covered the White House through seven presidents and was known to ask tough questions. Payne helped push civil rights issues to the forefront of national debate when she asked President Eisenhower when he planned to ban segregation in interstate travel. In 1964, President Lyndon Johnson invited Payne to witness his signing of the Civil Rights Act.

In 1972, Payne became the first Black female commentator on a national broadcast network when she was hired on the CBS program *Spectrum.*

Institutional affiliations

The *Chicago Defender*
White House Press Corps
CBS
Women's Institute for Freedom of the Press

Eye on the Struggle: Ethel Payne, the First Lady of the Black Press by James McGrath Morris (Amistad, 2015)

ZELDA JACKSON ORMES (ALSO KNOWN AS JACKIE ORMES)

August 1, 1917–December 26, 1985
Occupation: cartoonist, journalist, artist

Zelda "Jackie" Jackson Ormes was the first female African American cartoonist and the first to be nationally syndicated. She was born in Pittsburgh, Pennsylvania. Just out of high school, Ormes was hired as an editor and feature writer for the *Pittsburgh Courier*, a national Black newspaper. At the *Courier*, she created her first comic strip, *Torchy Brown in "Dixie to Harlem."* She published under the pen name "Jackie Ormes."

In 1942, Ormes moved to Chicago and started working for the **Chicago Defender** as a general assignment reporter. Her love of art drove her to produce her second daily cartoon, *Candy*, which featured the exploits of a clever-talking maid. Ormes went on to create *Patty-Jo 'n' Ginger*, a comic strip about a little girl and her sister that took on a number of social and political issues reflected in Black communities around the nation. The characters that Ormes created were heroines who challenged negative stereotypes about Black women and girls.

Patty-Jo 'n' Ginger ran in the *Defender* for eleven years, and Patty-Jo's character became the nation's first upscale African American doll. Ormes was also a member of multiple organizations, including the Chicago Urban League, the Windy City Press Club, and the **DuSable Museum of African American History.**

Chicago Defender
Pittsburgh Courier
DuSable Museum of African American History
Chicago Urban League
March of Dimes
Chicago Negro Chamber of Commerce
South Side Arts Center
Windy City Press Club
American Newspaper Guild
Urbanaides

Jackie Ormes: The First African American Woman Cartoonist by Nancy Goldstein (Ann Arbor: The University of Michigan Press, 2008)

IDA BELL WELLS-BARNETT AND FERDINAND LEE BARNETT'S FORMER RESIDENCE | 3624 S. King Drive

IDA BELL WELLS-BARNETT 🏠 🛠 ⚒ 🤝 👥 ✒ 🎓

July 16, 1862–March 25, 1931
Occupation: journalist, teacher, publisher, antilynching activist, suffragist, clubwoman

Born into slavery in Mississippi in 1862, Ida Bell Wells-Barnett was a teacher and later a famous journalist whose writing was a crusade against lynching and white terrorism. While she was working as a teacher in 1884, Wells-Barnett filed a lawsuit after being violently removed from a first-class seat on a train. She lost her case but was undeterred in her struggle for racial and gender justice.

When one of her close friends was lynched by a white mob in Memphis in 1892, Wells-Barnett wrote editorials encouraging Black people to leave the South and calling out the injustice of extrajudicial murders. In

retaliation for her writing, her newspaper's office was burned, and her life was threatened. Radicalized by this experience, Wells-Barnett embarked on an anti-lynching speaking tour in Great Britain. She also began to investigate racial terrorism in other parts of the United States, publishing some of her findings in a work titled *Southern Horrors: Lynch Law in All Its Phases*.

Wells-Barnett moved to Chicago in 1894 and eventually married Ferdinand Lee Barnett, a prominent Black lawyer and newspaper editor. From 1919 to 1929, Wells-Barnett and her family made their home at 3624 S. King Drive. She was the first Black adult probation officer in Chicago's municipal court. She campaigned for women's right to vote; led a delegation of Black women to Springfield, Illinois, in 1913 to lobby against racist legislation; and organized a campaign to elect a Black alderman in the Second Ward in 1914 and 1915. Wells-Barnett ran to be a delegate to the Republican National Convention in 1928 and for state senate in 1930.

Wells-Barnett helped to found several organizations, most notably the National Association of Colored Women and the National Association for the Advancement of Colored People (NAACP). She is one of the most important figures in nineteenth- and twentieth-century US history.

Institutional affiliations

Ida B. Wells Club

Alpha Suffrage Club

Negro Fellowship League

NAACP

Frederick Douglass Center Woman's Club

Chicago Political Equality League

Illinois Equal Suffrage Association

Conference of Women's Republican Clubs

Frederick Douglass Center

Additional landmarks and locations

The Light of Truth Ida B. Wells National Monument, 3729 S. Langley Avenue

Buried in Oak Woods Cemetery, 67th Street and Cottage Grove Avenue

Ida B. Wells Homes, 37th to 39th Streets between King Drive and Vincennes Avenue

Grace Presbyterian Church

More to read

Ida: A Sword Among Lions: Ida B. Wells and the Campaign Against Lynching by Paula J. Giddings (Harper, 2009)

ETTA MOTEN BARNETT'S HOME | 3619 S. King Drive

ETTA MOTEN BARNETT

November 5, 1901–January 2, 2004
Occupation: actress, singer, activist, philanthropist

Born on November 5, 1901, in Weimar, Texas, Etta Moten Barnett was a prominent singer and actress of stage and film known for her pathbreaking portrayals of Black women. She received acclaim for her performances in the 1933 films *Flying Down to Rio* (with Ginger Rogers and Fred Astaire) and *Gold Diggers of 1933*. The following year, she married Chicagoan Claude Barnett, founder of the Associated Negro Press. Moten Barnett was invited by First Lady Eleanor Roosevelt to sing at the White House in 1934, making her one of the first Black women to receive that honor. In 1942, she starred as Bess in the Broadway revival of *Porgy and Bess*, a role George Gershwin reportedly wrote with her in mind. "Before Halle Berry and Dorothy Dandridge and even Lena Horne, there was Etta Moten, a Black actress defying all the odds as an African American woman and performer," writes Joy Bennett Kinnon in *Ebony* magazine.

In 1952, vocal issues led Moten Barnett to stop performing. After her retirement from the stage, she actively supported and raised money for Chicago artistic, philanthropic, and social causes as well as national civic organizations. Her support work benefitted the **South Side Community Art Center**, the Lyric Opera of Chicago, the National Council of Negro Women, and her sorority, Alpha Kappa Alpha, among many other organizations. Moten Barnett also established a scholarship in her name for minority students at the Chicago Academy for the Performing Arts.

Harry Belafonte, who attended Moten Barnett's one-hundredth birthday party in Chicago, said she "gave Black people an opportunity to look at themselves on a big screen as something beautiful when all that was there before spoke to our degradation." Moten Barnett passed away in 2004, at the age of 102.

ORIGINAL HOME OF THE DUSABLE MUSEUM OF AFRICAN AMERICAN HISTORY (AND THE HOME OF MARGARET AND CHARLES BURROUGHS) | 3806 S. Michigan Avenue

MARGARET TAYLOR GOSS BURROUGHS
November 1, 1917-November 21, 2010
Occupation: artist, writer, poet, arts activist, founder

Dr. Margaret Burroughs's entire life was defined by education and art. Born in Louisiana, she moved to Chicago with her family during the Great Migration. She graduated from Englewood High School, going on to earn two degrees from the School of the Art Institute of Chicago and an art certificate from the art school La Esmeralda in Mexico City.

Burroughs taught at **DuSable High School**, in Illinois prisons, and as a college professor of art history for several decades. She was also a prolific writer who published fiction, multiple volumes of poetry, and children's books. As an artist, she created sculptures and paintings. Burroughs's work as a printmaker elevated the national profile of her artistry, and much of her artwork was acquired by renowned museums.

As an educator, Burroughs noticed the absence of African history as well as Black arts, cultural artifacts, and historical memory in schools. To address this deficiency, she and her husband Charles Gordon Burroughs started a museum on the first floor of their home at 3806 S. Michigan Avenue. Originally called the Ebony Museum of Negro History and Art, the museum has since been renamed the **DuSable Museum of African American History** in honor of Jean Baptiste Pointe DuSable, founder of the settlement that became the city of Chicago.

In its earliest inception, the DuSable Museum attracted hundreds of people to the Burroughses' home. What began as a grassroots initiative to uplift Black culture is now one of the oldest African American museums in the nation. Burroughs served as executive director of the museum for almost twenty-four years before retiring.

Burroughs's commitment to art and history reached beyond the museum. She was a cofounder of the National Conference of Artists (NCA), and a founder of the Lake Meadows Fair and the **South Side Community Art Center**.

Institutional affiliations

DuSable Museum of African American History
South Side Community Art Center
Art Institute of Chicago
National Conference of Artists (NCA)
Chicago Council on Fine Arts
National Commission on Negro History and Culture
Chicago Park District Board of Commissioners

Additional landmarks and locations

Margaret Burroughs Beach Park, 3100 S. Lake Shore Drive

SOUTH SIDE COMMUNITY ART CENTER
3831 S. Michigan Avenue

In 1940, **Margaret Taylor Goss Burroughs**, Eldzier Cortor, and a group of Chicago artists founded the South Side Community Art Center. They wanted to create a venue where Black artists would be able to create, perform, and display their talent for the community.

After a lengthy partnership between the group of artists, the Works Progress Administration, and the Federal Art Project of Illinois, in

combination with community-based fundraising efforts, the South Side Community Art Center opened at 3831 S. Michigan Avenue.

The South Side Community Art Center is considered the first Black art museum in the United States. Thousands of South Side residents gained access to free creative programs, art classes, writing workshops, exhibitions, and events through the center. Influential Black artists like Gordon Parks, Archibald Motley, and **Gwendolyn Brooks** frequented the center and displayed their work there. It became both a creative space for the arts and a political home for activists.

Eleanor Roosevelt, who was selected to dedicate the South Side Community Art Center in 1941, claimed in a column about the experience that the 1893 brownstone that housed the center was once the home of Charles Comiskey, founding owner of the White Sox.

In 1994, the center officially became a Chicago landmark. In 2017, it was named a national treasure by the National Trust for Historic Preservation. For over seventy-five years, the South Side Community Art Center has played a prominent role in the community as a Black arts institution and has provided creative resources to the adults and children of Chicago's South Side.

GWENDOLYN BROOKS'S FORMER RESIDENCE
4259 S. King Drive

GWENDOLYN BROOKS

June 7, 1917–December 3, 2000
Occupation: writer, poet, educator

Born in Topeka, Kansas, on June 7, 1917, Gwendolyn Brooks was a prolific and beloved writer and poet. She moved to Chicago as a baby and grew up on the South Side in Bronzeville. She began writing as a preteen and was published as a teenager in newspapers including the *Chicago Defender*. Brooks attended several high schools before finally graduating from Englewood High School. In 1945, she gained initial recognition for her collection of poems titled *A Street in Bronzeville*. In 1950, Brooks became the first Black writer to be awarded a Pulitzer Prize in literature, winning for her book *Annie Allen*. She served as the Illinois poet laureate for more than thirty years. Brooks was active in the Chicago Black Renaissance movement from the 1930s through the 1950s, and early in her career received encouragement from prominent writers including Langston Hughes and Richard Wright.

In 1931, Brooks and her new husband moved into a kitchenette apartment that still stands at 4259 S. King Drive. Constructed in 1893 when the neighborhood was white and wealthy, the building was originally called the Belmonte Flats. By the time Brooks arrived, the Belmonte Flats had been renamed the Tyson Apartments and carved up into tiny kitchenettes. Many unscrupulous white landlords—wanting to increase their profits and exploit Black people migrating to Chicago from the South—carved up single-family apartments into two or three smaller units, some of which didn't even have private bathrooms. This created cramped and substandard living conditions for thousands of Black people in Chicago. Brooks' poem "kitchenette building" tells the story of those crowded living quarters.

In 1967, Brooks wrote a commemorative poem for the dedication of a mural titled the *Wall of Respect*. The *Wall of Respect* at 43rd Street and Langley Avenue was painted that year by the Organization of Black American Culture, a collective of Black artists including many women. Myrna Weaver painted the "Sports" section, assisted by neighborhood resident and art student Florence Hawkins. **Barbara Jones-Hogu** painted the "Theater" section, and Carolyn Lawrence painted "Dance" on a nearby newsstand. Kathryn Akin painted a musician nearby. Brooks was depicted on the *Wall* in the "Literature" section. Other female heroes represented in the mural included Darlene Blackburn, Ruby Dee, Aretha Franklin, Billie Holiday, Claudia McNeil, the Marvelettes, Nina Simone, Cicely Tyson, Sarah Vaughan, and Dinah Washington. The *Wall of Respect* no longer exists.

Additional landmarks and locations

Gwendolyn Brooks Park is located at 4534-4540 S. Greenwood Avenue, less than a mile from Brooks' childhood home at 4332 S. Champlain Avenue.

From 1953 to 1994, Brooks lived at 7428 S. Evans Avenue.

More to read

A Surprised Queenhood in the New Black Sun: The Life & Legacy of Gwendolyn Brooks by Angela Jackson (Beacon Press, 2017)

MELISSA ANN ELAM HOME FOR WORKING WOMEN AND GIRLS | 4726 S. King Drive

MELISSA (OR MELISSIA) ANN ELAM 🏠 ⚒ ⚏
1853-1941
Occupation: settlement home founder, community organizer

Born enslaved in Missouri, Melissa Elam moved to Chicago after the Emancipation Proclamation was issued in 1863; there, she worked as a maid until she married a realtor named Ruben Elam. Elam noticed the lack of support for Black women moving into the city during the Great Migration—there was much concern that young women moving to Chicago had no defenses against moral corruption and threats to their safety. To address this issue, she opened the Melissa Ann Elam Home for Working Women and Girls in 1923. Elam encouraged the girls she housed to remain in school and later go into business. She wanted them to develop independence and economic preparedness.

The original Elam Home was located at 4555 S. Champlain Avenue on the South Side. In 1926, as the need for housing support grew, Elam purchased a mansion at 4726 S. King Drive. At its peak, the residence was home to over thirty women and girls. It was one of four homes in Chicago at the time that provided services specifically for Black women. The three-story home had twenty rooms, including a parlor, music room, and ballroom. It also served as a site of civic and social life during the 1920s and 1930s. In 1936, the State Con vention for Black Women was held in the home. **Ida Bell Wells-Barnett** was involved in the activities of the Elam Home. Melissa Ann Elam was, in turn, a member of Wells-Barnett's **Negro Fellowship League.**

When Elam passed away in 1941, her niece Lauretta Peyton gained ownership of the home. It was abandoned, and **Margaret Taylor Goss** **Burroughs** fought to make the home a Chicago landmark in 1979. It has since changed ownership and experienced a fire from which it has not recovered.

Institutional affiliations

Negro Fellowship League

COSMOPOLITAN COMMUNITY CHURCH | 5249 S. Wabash Avenue

MARY GREEN EVANS

January 13, 1891–April 12, 1966
Occupation: pastor, administrator

Born in Washington, DC, in 1891, Mary Green Evans was a community leader and pastor at the Cosmopolitan Community Church on Chicago's South Side. Evans challenged limitations on women's roles within the church and expanded the responsibilities of her church and its parishioners to the broader community.

Evans preached her first sermon at an African Methodist Episcopal (AME) church in Chicago at age twelve and received her bachelor's degree in divinity when she was twenty. She served as an evangelist, pastor, and accomplished fundraiser for the AME church until her move to become the second pastor of the Cosmopolitan Community Church in 1932.

Within four years of starting her position as pastor at the Cosmopolitan, Evans had eliminated the church's $36,000 debt and completely remodeled the facility. In 1948, she added "The House that Faith Built," a four-story building with a day nursery and kindergarten, health clinics, a kitchen, and a gym. In a first for an African American minister in Chicago, she based her financial stewardship of the church solely on tithing practices.

Evans was not only a preacher but also served as an independent pastor of her own congregation, at a time when it was not popular for women to do so. She worked diligently to implement educational, social, and health-related programming open to the entire community, regardless of church membership. During the Great Depression, the Cosmopolitan fed and clothed thousands of people. Evans created clubs whose members set aside money for specific projects in order to sustain those projects long-term. By 1963, she had finalized "The House that Love Built," a house for the aged, where she lived at the end of her life.

Because she never married and maintained two long-term relationships with women, there were persistent rumors that Evans was a lesbian. She never publicly confirmed or denied those rumors.

Although she rarely addressed social issues in her sermons, she did engage in civic action. The church ran a free medical clinic, maintained a rent fund, had a day nursery for working mothers, and formed a social service department. She was a supporter of the NAACP, particularly because of its antilynching campaigns. In 1942, Evans convinced 700 of her 826 parishioners to sign pledge cards to the NAACP.

Evans died in 1966. She was cremated, and her ashes were buried in the cornerstone of the Cosmopolitan Community Church.

LORRAINE HANSBERRY'S CHILDHOOD HOME
6140 S. Rhodes Avenue

LORRAINE HANSBERRY

May 19, 1930–January 12, 1965
Occupation: playwright, civil rights activist

Lorraine Hansberry was born at **Provident Hospital** in 1930. Her parents were activists, and her father, Carl Augustus Hansberry, founded one of the first Chicago banks to serve Black people. In 1937, Carl Hansberry bought a home at 6140 S. Rhodes Avenue in the all-white Woodlawn neighborhood. As Natalie Y. Moore writes in her book *The South Side* (2016), "When the family moved in, white mobs flung bricks through the windows, and one almost struck eight-year-old Lorraine. Her mother,

Nannie, a schoolteacher, patrolled the house at night with a gun." Neighbors went to court to challenge the Hansberrys' right to live in this previously all-white neighborhood, which was governed by a restrictive racial covenant. A legal battle ensued, during which the family were forced out of their home by an Illinois Supreme Court ruling. Subsequently, in a narrow technical ruling, the US Supreme Court found in favor of the Hansberrys. The decision didn't end the use of racially restrictive covenants, but it did open a thirty-block swath of the South Side to Black residents and paved the way for more decisive judgments against blatant housing discrimination. Hansberry would later draw on the experience to write the play *A Raisin in the Sun*.

During the period Hansberry attended Englewood High School, her family lived at 5936 S. Parkway Drive. Prominent Black artists and activists including Duke Ellington, W.E.B. Du Bois, Paul Robeson, and Langston Hughes frequented the home.

Hansberry's playwriting career began after she moved to New York in 1950 to work as a writer for Paul Robeson's progressive newspaper *Freedom*. Her play *A Raisin in the Sun* was the first Broadway play written by a Black woman when it opened in 1959. It won the prestigious New York Drama Critics Circle Award for best play, making Hansberry the first Black playwright and the youngest American playwright to win.

Lorraine married songwriter Robert Nemiroff in 1953. In 1965, she died of cancer at only thirty-four. Several of her plays and a collection of autobiographical writings were published after her death.

Additional landmarks and locations

5936 S. King Drive was Hansberry's teenage home.

Lorraine Hansberry Park is located at 5635 S. Indiana Avenue, fewer than two miles from Hansberry's childhood home in the Woodlawn community.

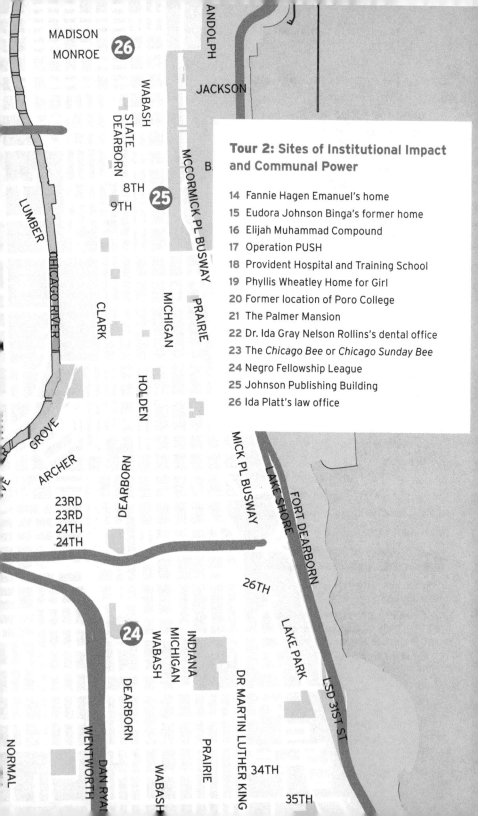

Tour 2: Sites of Institutional Impact and Communal Power

14 Fannie Hagen Emanuel's home
15 Eudora Johnson Binga's former home
16 Elijah Muhammad Compound
17 Operation PUSH
18 Provident Hospital and Training School
19 Phyllis Wheatley Home for Girl
20 Former location of Poro College
21 The Palmer Mansion
22 Dr. Ida Gray Nelson Rollins's dental office
23 The *Chicago Bee* or *Chicago Sunday Bee*
24 Negro Fellowship League
25 Johnson Publishing Building
26 Ida Platt's law office

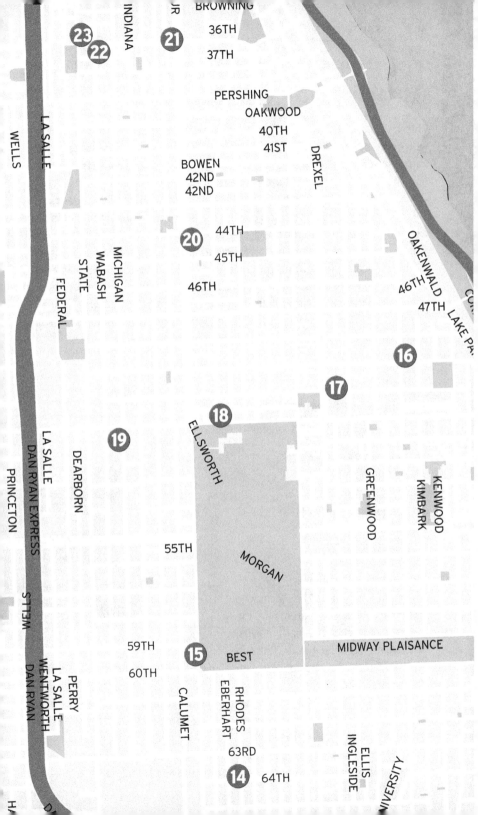

TOUR 2: SITES OF INSTITUTIONAL IMPACT AND COMMUNAL POWER

This tour highlights the vital role of community institutions and the women who built and upheld these sites of power. As hundreds of thousands of African Americans spilled into Chicago during the Great Migration, they faced a housing crisis, employment discrimination, and health care disparities. These women responded by building up institutions that sustained vital needs and served as pivotal neighborhood epicenters. The sites highlighted in this tour were developed by multifaceted creators. While they were building public spaces, they were also actively participating in multiple community organizations, collaborating with other local and national entities, and using their establishments to support political movements as well as the various needs of their constituents. Throughout this tour, readers can touch what remains of this history and experience the lasting impact of these women's legacies. (Note: this tour starts on the South Side and ends Downtown.)

FANNIE HAGEN EMANUEL'S HOME | 6352 S. Rhodes Avenue

FANNIE HAGEN EMANUEL

July 31, 1871–April 7, 1934
Occupation: settlement home founder, physician, clubwoman, community leader

Fannie Hagen Emanuel was born in Cincinnati, Ohio, in 1871. She moved to Chicago with her parents in the mid-1880s. During the early 1900s, when Black communities in Chicago experienced severe shortages of social service providers, settlement homes sought to fill the void. Emanuel founded the Emanuel Settlement House in 1908, which covered many of these needs on the South Side.

The settlement home gave Black children the opportunity to attend kindergarten classes that were otherwise only available to white children.

It offered a wide variety of class options for residents, including cooking, sewing, and art. The Emanuel House also provided vital services through its employment bureau, dental clinic, and youth activities.

The settlement house served as just one of Emanuel's many paths to community engagement. As a member of the Illinois Federation of Colored Women's Clubs, she was active across many issue areas. She also served on the board of directors of the Chicago Phyllis Wheatley Home, and became president of both the Frederick Douglass Center Woman's Club and the YWCA.

After the Emanuel Settlement House closed in 1912, Emanuel shifted her focus to obtaining a medical degree, starting medical school when she was forty-one years old. After graduating from the Chicago Hospital College of Medicine, she opened her own private medical practice, becoming one of the nation's few Black women physicians. Emanuel focused on providing medical services for Black women and girls.

Institutional affiliations

Ida B. Wells Women's Club
Illinois Federation of Colored Women's Clubs
Phyllis Wheatley Home
Frederick Douglass Center
YWCA
YMCA
Alpha Suffrage Club

Additional landmarks and locations

Emanuel Settlement House, 2732 W. Armour Avenue (now 2732 S. Federal Street)

EUDORA JOHNSON BINGA'S FORMER HOME
5922 S. King Drive

EUDORA JOHNSON BINGA

🏠 ✂ 💲 💡

February 22, 1871–March 26, 1933
Occupation: financial institution builder, entrepreneur, philanthropist

Eudora Johnson Binga was a wealthy Chicago socialite, businesswoman, and philanthropist. In 1907, she received a sizable inheritance from her brother, John "Mushmouth" Johnson—he had been a king of policy, a gambling enterprise where players placed bets on which numbers would be selected from a large wheel. In 1912, Eudora married Jesse Binga, a real estate mogul and former Pullman porter who had migrated to Chicago during the World's Fair of 1893 and planted roots. With their wealth, they started the House of Binga (renamed Binga State Bank), a private bank that served the Black community and provided an alternative to white-owned banks that met Black patrons with discrimination and predatory loans. In 1916, the couple funded the launch of *Champion Magazine*, billed as "a monthly survey of Negro achievement."

Binga's real estate properties created housing opportunities for Black families through blockbusting techniques—buying properties in white neighborhoods and renting to Black families. The influx of Black renters drove out white families, who then quickly sold their properties at very low prices. These practices, and the competition the Bingas' success posed to white businesses, led to violence from white neighbors. Binga properties, including the couple's home, were bombed eight times between 1917 and 1921. The Bingas also received threats after the Chicago Race Riots of July 1919, during which white mobs violently targeted Black Chicagoans, leading to a week of devastating violence.

Together, the Bingas used their legally and illegally accumulated wealth to create avenues for Black families to obtain housing, access loans, and create culture.

Institutional affiliations

House of Binga
Champion Magazine

Additional landmarks and locations

Binga State Bank, near State Street and 36th Street
Eudora Johnson Binga's childhood home, 5830 S. Wabash Avenue
Oak Woods Cemetery

ELIJAH MUHAMMAD COMPOUND
4847 S. Woodlawn Avenue

CLARA MUHAMMAD
November 2, 1899–August 12, 1972
Occupation: educator, institution builder

Clara Muhammad was born Clara Evans in Macon, Georgia, in 1899. Often referred to as the first lady of the Nation of Islam, she was an educator and the first wife of Nation of Islam leader Elijah Muhammad (1897–1975). She helped to support the organization for over ten years.

In 1923, Elijah Muhammad—born Elijah Poole in Georgia—moved his family to the developing auto city of Detroit, Michigan. The Great Depression hit Detroit and the nation hard, and people sought solutions to address the many social and economic problems that plagued the United States. It was during this period that Clara Muhammad began going to Wallace D. Fard's Temple of Islam. With her encouragement, her husband joined her, changed his name to Elijah Muhammad, and became Fard's chief disciple. When Fard disappeared, Elijah Muhammad became the head of the Nation of Islam and began to spread its message beyond Detroit. He encouraged his followers to take their children out of the public schools and enroll them in the Nation's developing school system. As a result, he began to be persecuted by the Detroit police and decided to leave Detroit for Chicago.

Arriving in Chicago in 1934 with Clara and their family, Elijah Muhammad established the new headquarters for the Nation of Islam and produced a newspaper, the *Final Call*, which followers were required to either buy or sell. Elijah refused to register for the draft in World War II and encouraged other members of the Nation to become conscientious objectors, leading to many of his followers being jailed; he himself was incarcerated in a federal prison in Milan, Michigan, from 1942 to 1946. During this period, the Nation of Islam began its prison ministry. Back in Chicago, Clara Muhammad led the organization and raised the couple's eight children alone during her husband's imprisonment.

Muhammad helped to establish and run the University of Islam and Muslim Girls Training schools. The first classes were in her home and took place once a week, with Muhammad as the first teacher. From the 1930s to the 1960s, the University of Islam provided Black children with "a worldview that stressed self-knowledge, self-reliance, and self-discipline" and pushed back against racist stereotypes about Black people. The university later moved to a former theater building.

The Muhammads withdrew their children from the public schools at a time when homeschooling was illegal. Clara Muhammad never returned her children to public school despite harassment by law enforcement. She told the police, "I would rather die than send my children to the public school system."

As a result of her leadership in education and the success of the University of Islam and Muslim Girls Training schools, the Nation of Islam went on to establish the Sister Clara Muhammad School System. There were over thirty-five schools in the continental United States and one school in Bermuda (Muhammad). Clara Muhammad passed away at the age of seventy-two from stomach cancer.

Additional landmarks and locations

Mosque Maryam (former location of Clara Muhammad Elementary School), 7351 S. Stony Island Avenue

OPERATION PUSH
930 E. 50th Street

WILLIE TAPLIN BARROW 💼 🛠 ⚒ 🤝 🕴
December 7, 1924–March 12, 2015
Occupation: community leader, civil rights activist, pastor

A lifelong civil rights leader known as "the Little Warrior," Reverend Willie Taplin Barrow marched with Martin Luther King Jr. and helped found the organization that became the Rainbow PUSH coalition in Chicago.

Born on December 7, 1924, in Burton, Texas, Barrow got her start fighting for racial equality long before she arrived in Chicago. In 1936, at only twelve years old, she led her first demonstration. Public schools were still segregated at the time, and Barrow and her Black classmates were forced to walk to school while white students were allowed to ride the bus. Barrow organized her fellow students to confront the bus driver and school officials. She later attended Warner Pacific Theological Seminary in Portland, Oregon, and helped build

a church in that city in the 1940s. She moved to Chicago's South Side with her husband Clyde Barrow in 1943.

Reverend Barrow advocated for women's and labor rights, worked to support affordable health care, and protested the Vietnam War. In later years, she also pushed for civil rights for the LGBT community. In Chicago during the mid-1960s, Barrow helped Jesse Jackson found Operation Breadbasket on the South Side to boost the economic power of Black Chicagoans. After that organization evolved into Rainbow PUSH, Barrow served as executive director of **Operation PUSH** for five years, the first woman to lead the organization. Barrow was named Chicago's woman of the year in 1969.

An author, activist, mentor, and

religious leader, Barrow never retired. She was often visible in the community as a guest speaker, at social events, and working at PUSH headquarters until her death on March 12, 2015, at the age of ninety.

PROVIDENT HOSPITAL AND TRAINING SCHOOL
500 E. 51st Street

Dr. Daniel Hale Williams founded Provident Hospital and Training School with the support of **Fannie Barrier Williams, Mary Jane Richardson Jones,** and other Black organizers in Chicago. At a time when few medical facilities provided adequate services to Black communities, Provident became the first Black operated, owned, and maintained hospital in the nation. In 1893, the nation's first successful open-heart surgery took place at Provident at the hands of Dr. Williams.

The hospital supported the needs of patients and provided opportunities for medical professionals in Chicago. Provident was also one of the only institutions to provide training for Black nurses. Its first home in 1891 was at 29th Street and Dearborn Street in a former meatpacking factory. Later it moved to 36th Street and Dearborn Street and expanded from twelve beds to sixty-five. In 1929, Provident relocated again to 51st Street and Vincennes Avenue. It became an affiliate of **Cook County Hospital** in 1974, and the current facility at 500 E. 51st Street opened in 1992.

FANNIE BARRIER WILLIAMS

February 12, 1855–March 4, 1944
Occupation: institution builder, orator,
political activist, organizer, women's
rights advocate, educator

After their marriage, Fannie Barrier Williams moved to Chicago with her husband S. Laing Williams. They both quickly became entrenched in the political movements building there. In 1891, Williams was one of the organizing forces behind the establishment of **Provident Hospital and Training School**. She went on to spend much of her life building institutions that would support the rights and resources of Chicago's South Side communities.

Williams's contributions to Chicago women's rights are extensive. She was an active member of the Illinois Women's Alliance and held multiple positions within the organization. She was also a founding member of the Phyllis Wheatley Club, the National League of Colored Women, and the National Association of Colored Women. In addition to Provident Hospital, she helped to establish the Frederick Douglass Center.

A powerful orator, Williams spoke out about the lack of representation of African Americans at the World's Columbian Exposition in 1893. During the exposition, she was among a small group of women selected to speak at the World's Parliament of Religions and stood before the World's Congress of Representative Women to give a presentation on the "intellectual progress of colored women in the United States since the Emancipation Proclamation."

Williams had many skills beyond community activism. She was a musician, reporter, and writer. She helped Booker T. Washington write his biography of Frederick Douglass. She also wrote several articles for publications including the *Chicago Record-Herald*, *New York Age*, and *Women's Era*.

Institutional affiliations

National League for the Protection of Colored Women

Chicago Women's Club

Chicago Public Library board

Phyllis Wheatley Club

National League of Colored Women

Illinois Women's Alliance

Chicago Women's Conference

Frederick Douglass Center

Chicago Political Equality League

Unitarian All Souls Church of Jenkin Lloyd Jones

Prudence Crandall Study Club

Institutional affiliations (continued)

Hyde Park Colored Voters
Republican Club

Taft Colored League

Black Diamond Development Company

Alliance Committee on State Schools
for Children

Abraham Lincoln Center

Chicago Woman's Club

National Association of Colored Women

National Negro Business League

More to read

*Fannie Barrier Williams: Crossing the
Borders of Region and Race* by Wanda
A. Hendricks (University of Illinois
Press, 2014)

CARRIE E. BULLOCK

June 16, 1887–December 31, 1962
Occupation: nurse, nursing leader

Born in South Carolina, Carrie E. Bullock received her nursing education from **Provident Hospital and Training School**, completing her training in 1909. Her career started with a position with the Chicago Visiting Nurse Association (VNA), where she provided medical attention to members of the Black community.

Bullock moved through the VNA in various capacities. She started as temporary staff, then became a staff nurse, and eventually an assistant supervisor. In 1919, she became the first Black nursing supervisor at the Chicago VNA. By the end of her forty-seven years of involvement with the VNA, Bullock had occupied every position within the association.

The National Association of Colored Graduate Nurses (NACGN) was established because Black nurses were denied membership in the American Nurses' Association. Bullock was elected vice president of the NACGN and was influential in raising money for initiatives that would directly benefit Black nurses. In a later stint as NACGN president, she created the *National News Bulletin*, a monthly publication that highlighted educational and career opportunities for nurses.

Even after retirement, Bullock continued her engagement in the profession by volunteering at Provident Hospital. She remained committed to public health throughout her life. Bullock worked for decades to provide direct medical services and increase educational resources for Black nurses, and she used her leadership positions to advance the field of nursing for generations to come. In 1938, the NACGN gave her the Mary Mahoney Award for outstanding achievement in nursing and human services.

Chicago Visiting Nurse Association
National Association of Colored Graduate Nurses
Grace Presbyterian Church

PHYLLIS WHEATLEY HOME FOR GIRLS
5128 S. Michigan Avenue

The Phyllis Wheatley Home was an outgrowth of the Phyllis Wheatley Women's Club, which was organized in 1896 in Chicago by writer and clubwoman Elizabeth Lindsay Davis. The home provided housing to young African American women who migrated to Chicago without local support. The first Phyllis Wheatley Home, started in 1908, was located at 3530 Forest Avenue. The second location was a brownstone at 3256 Rhodes Avenue, established in 1915. Next, the home expanded to the largest space yet, a three-story apartment building that housed up to twenty-two women, located at 5128 S. Michigan Avenue.

The Phyllis Wheatley Women's Club and Home is a part of the women's club movement that took place during the late nineteenth century and into the mid-twentieth century. The movement was born out of the dire need for social services—including housing, employment, education, and health care—for Black communities throughout the nation. In Chicago, Black women's clubs were the vehicle through which Black women organized to provide for and protect thousands of African Americans who poured into the city during the Great Migration.

Anti-lynching activist and journalist **Ida Bell Wells-Barnett** formed Chicago's first Black women's club in 1893. By 1920, there were over 150 Black women's clubs in the city and hundreds more nationally. These clubs and the women who organized them contributed to substantial political and social transformation during the Progressive Era. White women's clubs that formed before and during this era often excluded Black women and ignored the brutal conditions Black communities faced.

In response to violent racism and economic oppression, Black clubwomen built community institutions, led campaigns for legal representation, raised funds, and created youth programs, among a myriad of other endeavors. In 1896, the Federation of Afro-American Women and the Colored Women's League came together to form what would become known as the National Association of Colored Women's Clubs (NACWC).

ELIZABETH LINDSAY DAVIS

January 8, 1855–July 22, 1944
Occupation: clubwoman, writer, historian, educator

Elizabeth Lindsay Davis was a pioneer in the Black women's club movement, the founder of the **Phyllis Wheatley Home for Girls,** and a groundbreaking historian who documented the contributions of Black women organizers and writers.

The eldest daughter of Thomas Lindsay and Sophia Jane Lindsay, Davis was born in Peoria, Illinois, in 1855. After high school, she worked as a teacher in multiple states until she married chiropodist William H. Davis. The couple moved to Chicago in 1893.

Davis founded the second Black women's club in Chicago, the Phyllis Wheatley Club, and served as its president for twenty-eight years. The club's members created a home for African American girls that served as an essential establishment for those migrating to Chicago without economic support or housing options. In 1939, at eighty-four years old, Davis was featured in the *Chicago Defender,* encouraging the continued expansion of the home and the club.

Davis was also a charter member and national organizer for the National Association of Colored Women (NACW), the first Black national organization in the United States. Her leadership in this role led to the organization's expansion; by 1916, it had added nearly three hundred additional clubs. Davis later lent her organizing expertise to the Illinois Federation of Colored Women's Clubs as its fourth president.

A writer throughout much of her life, Lindsay wrote for several publications, including W. E. B. Du Bois's *The Crisis,* the *Chicago Defender,* and the NACW's *National Notes.* She is the author of *Illinois Federation of Colored*

Women's Clubs, 1900-1922 and the landmark text Lifting as They Climb. The two books are invaluable contributions to the historical record of Black women's social activism and the Black women's club movement.

As a political organizer, Davis advocated for women's suffrage and was a member of the Chicago Forum League of Women Voters. Interested in state and local politics, she joined the United States Council of National Defense and took a leadership role in the ward office for the Second Ward at the Frederick Douglass Center. She collaborated with prominent national organizers throughout her life, including **Ida Bell Wells-Barnett** and W. E. B. Du Bois.

Institutional affiliations

League of Women Voters
Women's Aid
Chicago Council of Defense
NACW
Illinois Federation of Colored Women's Clubs
Illinois Association of Women's Clubs
Frederick Douglass Center
The Phyllis Wheatley Home Association
Women's City Club
Gaudeamus Charity Club

Additional landmarks and locations

Former home, 3226 S. Prairie Avenue

MARY FITZBUTLER WARING

November 1, 1869-December 3, 1958
Occupation: physician, educator, activist, clubwoman, writer

Mary Fitzbutler Waring was an influential physician, educator, and activist who expanded health care for Black communities. Born in 1869 in Canada, Waring grew up with a family of physicians at a time when there were few Black men and women in the medical field. Her parents, Sarah and Henry Fitzbutler, were both doctors engaged in community health work. The family moved to the US, and Waring was raised in Kentucky.

After graduating from high school, Waring was trained as a teacher at a normal school and then attended Louisville National Medical College, receiving her degree in 1898. In 1901, she married educator and high school principal Frank Waring. The two moved to Chicago, where she started a career as a teacher at **Wendell Phillips Academy High School**. Waring eventually returned to the medical field and graduated from the Medical College of Chicago in 1923.

Waring was involved with Chicago clubwomen and community

organizations providing social services for Black women, youth, and mothers. She became president of the Necessity Club and provided childcare support through the development of the club's day nursery. Waring also worked with the Emanuel Settlement Day Nursery and was a member of the **Phyllis Wheatley Home for Girls**. She took on several leadership roles in the NACW, including becoming the chair of its Department of Health and Hygiene. In 1913, she sponsored training sessions and health programs in response to a national tuberculosis epidemic, aware that nutrition and sanitation were more often available to wealthier white communities.

Waring often wrote in the NACW's *National Notes* in hopes of spreading awareness about the extreme disparities in providing health services. Working with the National Nurse Training Service, she also organized training classes for nurses. As another part of her regional organizing, she implemented home care classes in St. Louis, Missouri.

Between 1930 and 1937, Waring served as vice president and then president of the NACW. She used her office to advocate for economic justice and employment opportunities for Black women and Black communities in general. Alongside work with the NACW, Waring was a speaker for the National Women's Anti-Lynching League and an active member of organizations including the Chicago League of Women Voters, the National Republican League of Colored

Women, Delta Sigma Theta Sorority, and the NAACP.

Institutional affiliations

Emanuel Settlement Day Nursery
Necessity Club
National Republican League of Colored Women
Chicago League of Women Voters
NAACP
Red Cross
National Nurse Training Service
Delta Sigma Theta Sorority
Illinois Federation of Colored Women's Clubs
Wendell Phillips Academy High School
National Women's Anti-Lynching League
NACW

Additional landmarks and locations

Former home, 4557 S. Michigan Avenue

FORMER LOCATION OF PORO COLLEGE
Mollison Elementary School, 4415 S. King Drive

Poro College, a block-long complex that housed entrepreneur **Annie Minerva Turnbo Malone**'s hair care company, relocated to Chicago after over a decade in St. Louis, Missouri. The complex included housing facilities as well as educational spaces, business offices, a performance hall, laboratories, and a rooftop garden.

The new "Poro Block" spanned from 4401 to 4427 South Parkway, which is now known as King Drive. Beyond serving as the company's headquarters, Poro College was a gathering space for communities on the South Side and served as a meeting space for groups including the Chicago Urban League and the NAACP.

ANNIE MINERVA TURNBO MALONE

August 9, 1869–May 10, 1957
Occupation: inventor, entrepreneur, institution builder

Annie Minerva Turnbo Malone was born in Metropolis, Illinois, on August 9, 1869. Her parents were born into slavery and died while she was young. Turnbo Malone was raised by her older siblings in Metropolis and later in Peoria.

Turnbo Malone was regularly sick and unable to attend school, so she didn't graduate. However, she cultivated her love and knowledge of chemistry and practiced hairdressing with her sister, developing the skills that led her to start her business. By age twenty, Turnbo Malone had created a shampoo and scalp treatment for Black women. She sold and marketed her products on a buggy while making speeches, giving demonstrations, and offering free samples.

In 1902, Turnbo Malone decided to move to St. Louis to reach a larger market and promote her "Wonderful Hair Grower" products in the city with the fourth-largest Black population in the country. As a Black businesswoman, she didn't have access to the regular distribution channels and instead gave door-to-door demonstrations. Her beauty products were exhibited in the World's Trade Fair of 1904. The fact that Wonderful Hair Grower did not damage the hair or scalp like many comparable products of that time led to much of the brand's success. In 1904, Turnbo Malone opened her first shop, and by 1906 she had trademarked her brand as Poro. Turnbo Malone's business kept expanding, and by 1918 it was worth over one million dollars.

That same year, Poro's success led Turnbo Malone to build a four-story, million-dollar factory and college that employed over 175 people and created educational and employment opportunities for young Black women. **Poro College** became a nationwide endeavor as the brand grew. In 1930, Turnbo Malone relocated Poro's headquarters to Chicago, where it took up a city block. This headquarters was listed in the Green Book, a book for Black travelers who sought out safe and welcoming sleeping quarters and dining venues while traveling throughout the US in the era of Jim Crow. The current Irvin C. Mollison Elementary School sits on the block where the Poro Headquarters once existed.

Turnbo Malone described Poro as an "industrial effort of the colored people, by the colored people, for the colored people." She was one of the earliest and most successful Black beauty culture entrepreneurs, and by the 1920s she was one of the country's wealthiest Black women. She was also a major philanthropist, donating to orphanages across the country and raising funds to construct the St. Louis Colored Orphans' Home. She donated to African American churches as well as community organizations like the YMCA. Turnbo Malone also supported higher learning institutions and financed education for two full-time students in every historically Black college and university in the United States.

Institutional affiliations

World's Trade Fair
YMCA
Colored Women's Federated Clubs of St. Louis
National Negro Business League
Commission on Interracial Cooperation
Republican Party
AME Church
Zeta Phi Beta Sorority

THE PALMER MANSION | 3654 S. King Drive

Architect William Wilson Clay designed the Palmer Mansion, which was built between 1885 and 1888, for D. Harry Hammer, a Chicago attorney, alderman, and Cook County judge. In 1976, the home was purchased by Chicago activists Jorja and Lu Palmer, who would live there for nearly three decades.

After the Palmers passed away, the mansion was vacant for fourteen years; Preservation Chicago named it one of "Chicago's Most Endangered Buildings" in 2019, warning that it faced "demolition by neglect." In 2021, The Obsidian Collection, a nonprofit run by Bronzeville native Angela Ford that is dedicated to archiving Black historical media and making it publicly accessible, purchased the 133-year-old mansion with the vision of converting it into a multi-use space that will include a museum and library.

JORJA ENGLISH PALMER ⚒ 🗂 🤝
June 16, 1930–December 9, 2005
Occupation: political activist, institution builder, community organizer, strategist

Jorja English Palmer founded Illinois's first group home for African American children, the Stanford English Home for Boys. She organized alongside Martin Luther King Jr. and

hosted one of the largest-ever voter registration drives in Illinois as part of the effort to elect Harold Washington as Chicago's first Black mayor. As a longtime community activist, political strategist, and organizer, she fought for housing rights, education access, and voting rights, and against police brutality.

Palmer was born in New Madrid, Missouri. After tragically losing her mother and father at a young age, she and her siblings were moved to Chicago to be cared for by relatives. Palmer attended **DuSable High School**; there, she first became engaged in community organizing when her teachers sent her to participate in NAACP Youth Council meetings. She went on to attend the University of Illinois at Navy Pier. In 1950, she married Jamie English, whom she later divorced.

In the 1960s, Palmer held a leadership role in the West Chatham Improvement Organization Education Committee and organized a historic boycott against "Willis wagons." Named after superintendent Benjamin Willis, Willis wagons were cramped, temporary mobile classrooms used to keep Black children out of white neighborhood schools. The boycott was successful in getting rid of both Superintendent Willis and his wagons. Palmer's efforts to end school segregation led her and other activists to found the Coordinating Council of Community Organizations. It was through this organization that she organized for fair housing alongside Dr.

Martin Luther King Jr.

Teaming up with activist and journalist Lu Palmer, Congressman Ralph Metcalf, and attorney Thomas Todd to fight police brutality in the seventies, Palmer helped to form the Black Crime Commission. She would go on to marry Lu Palmer in 1975. Together, the Palmers were a powerful organizing force in the Chicago South Side community. Their massive voter-registration drive helped Harold Washington run and win the race to become the mayor of Chicago. The Palmers also founded Chicago Black United Communities, the Black Independent Political Organization, and the Lu Palmer Foundation.

In addition to her organizing and community-building work, Jorja led political education classes at **Malcolm X College** in 1982. That same year, she established the Stanford English Home for Boys, named after her son, who was diagnosed with autism and required extensive care. The facility was Illinois's first group home for African American children.

In 2005, after her death from cancer, the Illinois Senate issued a resolution to acknowledge Palmer as a freedom fighter and longtime community activist.

Additional landmarks and locations

The Garvey Center at 330 E. 37th Street is the coach house behind the **Palmer Mansion**, where two of the Palmer's organizations, Chicago Black United Communities and the Black Independent Political Organization, still operate.

Institutional affiliations

Stanford English Home for Boys	Operation PUSH
Chicago Community Council Improvement Organization	Garfield Organization
	Black Panther Party
Student Nonviolent Coordinating Committee	Chicago Urban League
	Lu Palmer Foundation
NAACP	Malcolm X College
Congress of Racial Equality	DuSable High School

DR. IDA GRAY NELSON ROLLINS' DENTAL OFFICE
3652 S. Wabash Avenue

Ida Gray Nelson Rollins established multiple dentist office locations over the course of her nearly forty year career. Her first dental office in Chicago was located at Armour Avenue and 35th Street, but by 1898, she had closed it and opened one in her home at 3558 S. State Street. Seven years later, she moved her practice and home to S. Wabash Ave. Rollin's office was on the first floor of 3654 S. Wabash. She maintained her practice until she retired in the 1930s. Her home was on the second floor at 3652 S. Wabash, where she lived for the rest of her life.

IDA GRAY NELSON ROLLINS

💼 🗂 👥 ❖

February 20 or March 4, 1867–May 3, 1953
Occupation: doctor of dental surgery, community organizer, institution builder, clubwoman

Ida Gray Nelson Rollins was a trail-blazing dentist. She was born in Clarksville, Tennessee, but grew up in Cincinnati, Ohio after her mother died when Rollins was an infant. In Cincinnati, Rollins attended a segregated public school and worked as a seamstress. In 1887, she began studies at the University of Michigan School of Dentistry, and in 1890, she became

the first Black woman with a doctor of dental surgery degree (DDS).

Rollins started a private dental practice in Cincinnati and later relocated to Chicago after her 1895 marriage to James Sanford Nelson. Rollins reportedly served both Black and white clients. In addition to practicing dentistry, she was involved in several community initiatives. She mentored other Black women in dentistry and even inspired one of her patients, Olive Myrtle Henderson, to become the second Black woman to practice the profession in Chicago. Rollins was also vice president of the Eighth Regiment Ladies Auxiliary, which secured necessary supplies such as bed linens for hospitals, and vice president of the Phyllis Wheatley Club.

Rollins retired in 1928 and remarried in 1929. She died in Chicago in 1953. The School of Dentistry at the University of Michigan has established an annual diversity award in her honor.

Institutional affiliations

Professional Women's Club of Chicago
Eighth Regiment Ladies Auxiliary
Phyllis Wheatley Club
University of Michigan School of Dentistry

THE *CHICAGO BEE* OR *CHICAGO SUNDAY BEE*
Chicago Bee Branch Library, 3647 S. State Street

In 1926, businessman Anthony Overton founded the *Chicago Bee* or *Chicago Sunday Bee*, a Black newspaper with an almost entirely female staff. Based at 3647 S. State Street on Chicago's South Side, the *Bee*'s editors included **Ida Bell Wells-Barnett** and **Olive Myrl Diggs**, who conceived of the newspaper as "an agent of change."

Writing about the *Bee*, historian Anne Meis Knupfer suggests that the paper demonstrated "a steadfast focus on the connections among literature, art, history, and politics." For example, the *Bee* published its "Labor News" and "Art Notes" columns side by side. **Gwendolyn Brooks**' first published poems appeared in the *Bee*, and subscribers could read weekly installments of Richard Wright's *Native Son* or order the novel directly from the newspaper's book department.

The *Bee* sponsored the original "Mayor of Bronzeville" contest, which led to the use of the term "Bronzeville" for the neighborhood. The expression was originally suggested by theater editor James Gentry, who coined the term and had been sponsoring a beauty contest in the neighborhood since 1916. When Gentry left the *Bee* in 1932, he took the term with him to the ***Chicago Defender***, which continued the contests.

OLIVE MYRL DIGGS

Lifespan Dates: unknown-d. 1980
Occupation: journalist, administrator, public servant

Olive Myrl Diggs, a journalist and socialite, worked her way up to become managing editor of the ***Chicago Bee***. A graduate of Northwestern University and Roosevelt University, Diggs began as the *Bee*'s editor (1929–1930) and later served as its business manager (1930–1934). In 1937, she began her tenure as managing editor, which ran until the paper folded in 1947. After the *Bee* closed, Diggs became acting director of the Illinois Commission on Human Relations, and later worked in the Department of Urban Renewal, writing about and speaking on public housing in Chicago.

MARIAN CAMPFIELD

Lifespan Dates: unknown
Occupation: journalist, editor

Throughout the 1930s and 1940s, Marian Campfield was the city editor of the ***Chicago Bee***. She was responsible for the paper's general reporting and focused a lot of attention on women's issues. In 1947, when the *Bee* closed, Campfield became women's editor at the ***Chicago Defender***.

NEGRO FELLOWSHIP LEAGUE
Dearborn Homes, 2830 S. State St.

The Negro Fellowship league location moved from: 2830 S. State Street (1910-1913) to 3005 S. State Street (1913-1915). Both locations have since been demolished. 2830 S. State Street (pictured here) is the current site of the Dearborn Homes housing complex.

The Negro Fellowship League (NFL) was founded in 1908 by **Ida Bell Wells-Barnett** and a group of students from her Bible study class. Wells-Barnett built the organization into a reading room and social center, which moved into a rented space at 2830 S. State Street in 1910. Jessie Lawson, wife of Victor Lawson, the owner of the *Chicago Daily News*, provided seed money to finance the move and establish early programming. Wells-Barnett biographer Mia Bay describes the activities of the NFL reading room in her book, *To Tell the*

Truth Freely: The Life of Ida B. Wells:

> Staffed by one employee and a roster of volunteers, the NFL's reading room was open from 9 a.m. to 10 p.m., and housed a "selected library of history, biography, fiction and race literature especially." It offered visitors a place to read, study, write letters, and pursue a "quiet game of checkers, dominoes or other games that would not interfere with those who wished to read." Nonalcoholic refreshments were available... Visitors were also encouraged to attend weekly lectures by a variety of prominent speakers, ranging from white reformers such as Jane Addams and Mary White Ovington to black intellectuals such as William Monroe Trotter, Garland Penn, and the historian Carter G. Woodson. Free and open to the public, these events attracted local people as well as league members.

However, the NFL was much more than just a reading room and social center. It began to offer lodging to young men who had just migrated to Chicago—visitors could rent a bed for fifty cents a night. The NFL offered food to those in need and helped people find employment. In its first year of operation, the employment bureau placed 115 men in jobs.

The NFL provided support to prisoners, working to protect Black men from injustice. This focus seemed most important to Wells-Barnett. She and her husband worked through the NFL to represent many young Black men who had been falsely accused of crimes and to secure the release of individuals who had been convicted.

Wells-Barnett was able to secure individual contributions and some grant funding for the first couple years of the NFL's existence, but from 1913 until 1916, she sustained the organization with the $150/month salary she received from her work as a probation officer. The NFL had to close its doors in 1920 due to lack of funding.

More to read

To Tell the Truth Freely: The Life of Ida B. Wells by Mia Bay (Hill and Wang, 2009)

JOHNSON PUBLISHING BUILDING | 820 S. Michigan Avenue

This eleven-story building on South Michigan Avenue, which served for decades as the corporate headquarters of the Johnson Publishing Company, is often referred to as the *"Ebony/Jet* Building." Designed by John Moutoussamy and built in the early 1970s, it was the first—and, as of 2022, remains the only—downtown Chicago high-rise designed by an African American architect.

In 2017, the building gained city landmark status, which protects the exterior and the large *Ebony/Jet* sign from being removed, destroyed, or significantly altered. The high-rise home of the former African American publishing empire was vacant for several years before Chicago's Columbia College bought the property. They then sold it to 3L Real Estate; it has since been converted into an apartment building.

EUNICE WALKER JOHNSON

April 4, 1916–January 3, 2010
Occupation: businesswoman,
institution builder, fashion
entrepreneur, philanthropist

Eunice Walker Johnson was a fashion pioneer who founded and directed Ebony Fashion Fair and Fashion Fair Cosmetics, partnering with her husband to establish the Johnson Publishing Company empire.

Born Eunice Walker in Salem, Alabama, Johnson came from a prominent family. Her father, Nathaniel Walker, was a doctor, and her mother, Ethel Walker, was a high school principal and college professor. Johnson received her undergraduate degree from Talladega College in Alabama and then moved to Chicago, where she earned a master's degree from Loyola University. In Chicago, she met John H. Johnson; the two married in 1941, not long after she graduated from Loyola.

While many accounts mention John H. Johnson as the sole founder of Johnson Publishing company, Eunice was a partner and creative director alongside her husband. In 1942, the couple created *Negro Digest* together in the style of *Reader's Digest*. The success of the *Digest* led them to create *Ebony*, a monthly magazine about Black life with a photo-centered design that resembled that of *Life* magazine. Eunice Johnson is credited with conceiving the name for the magazine.

In 1958, Johnson organized a fashion show to help raise funds for a New Orleans hospital. This philanthropic endeavor evolved into Ebony Fashion Fair, an annual fashion tour that garnered international acclaim for over fifty years. The fair was a global platform that helped to develop the careers of prominent African American models and designers and raised millions of dollars for community development, education, and civil rights organizations.

Johnson expanded her reach into beauty products, founding Fashion Fair Cosmetics. The company reached customers around the world at a time when there were very few options for makeup designed explicitly for Black women. Fashion Fair Cosmetics became one of the largest Black-owned cosmetic companies.

In 2010, Johnson passed away in her Chicago home at the age of ninety-three. While the Johnson Publishing Company has since dissolved, Fashion Fair Cosmetics continues to thrive.

ERA BELL THOMPSON 📖✏️

August 10, 1905–December 30, 1986
Occupation: writer, editor, journalist

Era Bell Thompson was an important journalist and literary figure in the Chicago Black Renaissance movement. She was born in Des Moines, Iowa, in 1905; in 1914, her family moved to Dakota Territory. When Thompson was twelve years old, her mother suddenly died; her father, who had been born into slavery, continued to raise her himself along with her older brothers. They were the only Black family in their city of Driscoll, North Dakota.

Thompson was a star track-and-field athlete at the University of North Dakota but had to leave after two years; she later graduated from Morningside College in Iowa with a degree in journalism. Thompson attended Morningside under the direction of its then-president Dr. Robert E. O'Brian, a white man whose family adopted her for a period while she finished her studies. Thompson wrote about the complexities of her experience with the O'Brian family in her autobiography *American Daughter*.

In 1933, Thompson moved to Chicago, where she started working as a housekeeper. She was then hired to write for the **Chicago Defender** but continued to work odd jobs to supplement her income. Thompson wrote for the *Defender* under the pseudonym Dakota Dick, whom she described as "a bad, bad cowboy from the wild and wooly West." In her dissertation, literary scholar Eileen De Freece-Wilson

argues that Thompson's work used "humor as a radical means to shift the language of thinking about race."

Thompson was hired by the Works Progress Administration, and in 1945 won a Newberry Fellowship that allowed her to finish *American Daughter*. She continued her studies in a graduate-level journalism program at Northwestern University. Thompson held multiple prominent editorial positions over the course of her career, first at the *Negro Digest*, then as a pioneering photojournalist and managing editor for *Ebony* magazine. She would go on to become the magazine's international editor. Thompson worked with the Johnson Publishing Company until her retirement.

Her success as a literary figure, which began with the publication of *American Daughter*, earned her many honors and accolades. Thompson's writing often included distinguished public figures such as **Edith Spurlock**

Sampson, Joe Louis, **Gwendolyn Brooks**, and Langston Hughes. Her second book, *Africa, Land of My Fathers*, published in 1954, is about her travels through multiple African countries. Throughout her life, Thompson traveled around the world, visiting over 120 countries.

Thompson was also involved in various organizations, including the NAACP; she was a member of the Board of Directors of the Chicago YWCA and of the literary advisory committee of the **George C. Hall Branch of the Chicago Public Library**. She left behind an archive of papers that is now housed at the Vivian G. Harsh Research Collection at the Carter G. Woodson Branch of the Chicago Public Library.

Institutional affiliations

Ebony
NAACP
University of Chicago Press
Chicago Defender
Johnson Publishing Company
Negro Digest
Hall Library
Newberry Fellowship
Northwestern University
Chicago YWCA

Additional landmarks and locations

Prairie Shore Apartments, 2851 S. Martin Luther King Drive
George C. Hall Branch of the Chicago Public Library, 4801 S. Michigan Avenue

IDA PLATT'S LAW OFFICE
36 S. State Street
(formerly 40 S. State Street)

IDA PLATT 🏠 ⚒
1863–unknown
Occupation: lawyer

Born in Chicago, Ida Platt was the first Black woman to earn an Illinois law license (in 1894) and the third Black woman lawyer in the nation. She was descended from a line of free and affluent Black people, the youngest of eight children. In 1854, Platt's parents moved to Chicago from New York. When her father died in 1888, he left his family a fortune estimated at $50,000 to $100,000.

Platt attended Central High School, an integrated public school in Chicago, where she studied French and German and graduated at age sixteen. After working in the insurance industry for nine years, Platt decided to attend law school. She was admitted to the bar after graduation and remained the only Black woman lawyer in Illinois until 1920.

Platt never publicly claimed a Black identity, and unlike other early Black Chicago settlers, she never participated in any racial uplift activities. After both of her parents died, she seemingly changed her racial identity to white; her very light skin and features allowed her to pass. In 1928, at sixty-five years old, Platt disappeared from the city and its legal directories. There is speculation that she married and moved to England.

Institutional affiliations

Women's Bar Association of Illinois

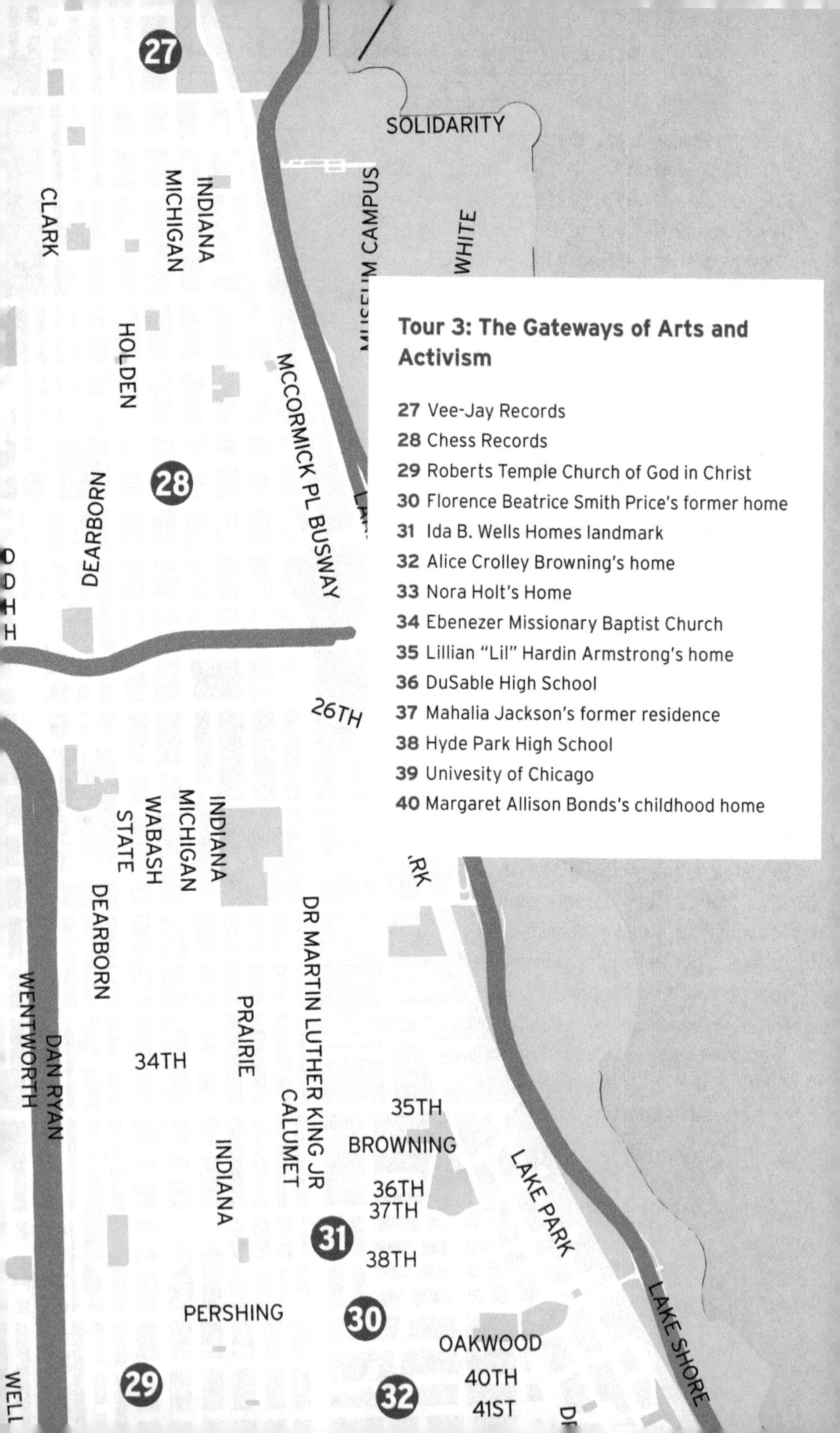

27

SOLIDARITY

CLARK

INDIANA
MICHIGAN

MUSEUM CAMPUS

WHITE

HOLDEN

McCORMICK PL BUSWAY

28

DEARBORN

Tour 3: The Gateways of Arts and Activism

27 Vee-Jay Records
28 Chess Records
29 Roberts Temple Church of God in Christ
30 Florence Beatrice Smith Price's former home
31 Ida B. Wells Homes landmark
32 Alice Crolley Browning's home
33 Nora Holt's Home
34 Ebenezer Missionary Baptist Church
35 Lillian "Lil" Hardin Armstrong's home
36 DuSable High School
37 Mahalia Jackson's former residence
38 Hyde Park High School
39 Univesity of Chicago
40 Margaret Allison Bonds's childhood home

26TH

INDIANA
MICHIGAN
WABASH
STATE

DEARBORN

DR MARTIN LUTHER KING JR

CALUMET

.RK

DAN RYAN

WENTWORTH

34TH

PRAIRIE

INDIANA

35TH

BROWNING

LAKE PARK

36TH
37TH

31

38TH

PERSHING

30

OAKWOOD

LAKE SHORE

WELL

29

32

40TH
41ST

TOUR 3: THE GATEWAYS OF ARTS AND ACTIVISM

The profound connection between the arts and activism is deeply rooted in Chicago. Throughout the city's history, the creative brilliance of Black women's artistry has intersected with the impact of their political strategy to generate community transformation. Here, we chart the lives of women who used their skills to create portals of change for the city and nation. Many of the artists profiled were pushing against racial barriers in their respective fields while using their art to highlight issues of civil rights and social justice. In tandem, Black women activists were engaged in innovative tactics to garner resources, support, and awareness of ongoing injustices. Using words, dance, music, and collective force, these activists and artists help to shape many Chicago neighborhoods. Through this tour, walk in the shoes of the women who moved the city and nation forward in unique and beautiful ways.

VEE-JAY RECORDS
1449 S. Michigan Avenue

Vee-Jay Records, once the largest Black-owned record company in the United States, was originally located at 2129 S. Michigan Avenue across the street from Chess Records. The company later moved to its more well-known location at 1449 S. Michigan Avenue.

VIVIAN CARTER 🔧💡
March 25, 1921–June 12, 1989
Occupation: disc jockey, record company owner

In 1953, Vivian Carter and her husband James Bracken founded **Vee-Jay Records.** Vee-Jay was the largest

Black-owned record company in the United States prior to the founding of Motown. The company saw immediate success, with its first song reaching the top of the national rhythm-and-blues charts. In less than a decade, Vee-Jay expanded to produce in the pop, jazz, and soul genres, becoming one of the first multimillion-dollar Black-owned recording companies in the nation. Renowned artists including Gladys Knight & the Pips, Little Richard, Jerry Butler and the Impressions, the Dells, and the Beatles were among the talent discovered by the record label.

CHESS RECORDS | 2120 S. Michigan Avenue

KOKO TAYLOR 💼 🛠 ✏
September 28, 1935–June 3, 2009
Occupation: singer, musician

Nicknamed the "Queen of Chicago Blues," Koko Taylor was a musical icon and one of the most revered female blues vocalists of her time. She made her name in Chicago's tough electric blues scene during the early 1960s.

Born Cora Walton on September 28, 1935, in Memphis, Tennessee, Taylor found her passion for music from singing in church choir and while working in the cotton fields. Her family loved music, and Taylor often sang while her brothers played handmade instruments. Taylor lost both of her parents at a young age; her mother died when she was only four years old, and her father passed away when she was eleven. She left school in the sixth grade and only returned to night school in Chicago many years later.

Taylor and her husband, Robert "Pops" Taylor, moved to Chicago in the 1950s. Pops encouraged Taylor to begin singing with blues bands at various South Side clubs. She was discovered by musician and record producer Willie Dixon, who played an instrumental role in launching her career. Taylor received her first contract with Chess Records in 1965. The blues legend often wrote her own material, drawing on everyday lived experiences. She once declared, "It's tough being out there doing what I'm doing in what they call a man's world!" She was influenced by blues artists Bessie Smith, Big Mama Thornton, and Memphis Minnie, and is credited with influencing singers such as Janis Joplin and Bonnie Raitt.

In the 1990s, Taylor appeared in the films *Blues Brothers 2000* and *Wild at Heart*. She opened a blues club on Division Street in Chicago's South Loop in 1994.

ROBERTS TEMPLE CHURCH OF GOD IN CHRIST
4021 S. State Street

JUANITA "ARIZONA" DRANES

1889 or 1891–1963
Occupation: pianist, singer

Very little is known about the childhood of blind gospel musician Arizona Dranes. She was born in either 1889 or 1891 in Texas, the youngest of three children, and was classically trained in voice and piano starting at age seven. In 1912, she graduated from the Deaf, Dumb, and Blind Institute for Colored Youth in Austin, Texas. In 1926, Dranes traveled to Chicago to record music for OKeh Records. Dranes moved to Chicago in 1929 and spent a few years playing music at **Roberts Temple Church of God in Christ**, where an eleven-year-old Rosetta Tharpe first heard her. After 1928, she never recorded again but continued to sing and play music across the nation. Though largely forgotten today, Dranes is a gospel music pioneer. She died in 1963 in California.

MAMIE TILL-MOBLEY

November 23, 1921–January 6, 2003
Occupation: civil rights activist

In August 1955, Emmett Till, a fourteen-year-old Black boy from Chicago visiting family in Mississippi, was accused by a white woman of having whistled at her in a grocery store. Three days later, Till was dragged out of bed in the dead of night, brutally beaten, and then shot to death by at least two white men. After his murder, Till's body was dumped in the Tallahatchie River. Although his killers were arrested and charged, both were quickly acquitted by an all-white, all-male jury. Shortly thereafter, the defendants sold their story to a journalist, including a detailed account of how they lynched Till.

Emmett's mother, Mamie Till, was born in Mississippi, but grew up in Argo, Illinois. She married Louis Till when she was eighteen, and her son, Emmett, was born a year later. She soon separated from her husband and moved with her son to the South

Side of Chicago. In 1955, when she sent Emmett for a summer visit to her relatives in Mississippi, she could not have imagined the tragedy that would befall him. Till insisted on giving her son an open-casket funeral and allowed photographs of his body to be published in the Black press so everyone could witness the brutality of his unjust murder. Till's provocative decision helped ignite the spark which fueled the modern Civil Rights Movement in the US.

Emmett Till's funeral was held at **Roberts Temple Church of God in Christ**. More than fifty thousand people viewed Emmett's body. At the time, the church was pastored by Reverend Isaiah Roberts, son of the church's founder and one of the major figures in the development of Pentecostalism in Chicago. A host of

ministers from different denominations representing the major Black churches in the city presided over the funeral. Among them were Archibald Carey Jr. of Quinn Chapel and Bishop Louis Henry Ford, another of the major figures in the history of the Pentecostal church after whom the Bishop Ford Highway is named.

After her son's lynching, Mamie Till-Mobley continued to speak out against racial terrorism while galvanizing support for the NAACP. In 1988, Emmett Till's accuser admitted that she had lied.

Additional landmarks and locations

Mamie Till-Mobley Park is located at 6404 S. Ellis Avenue, only blocks from where Mamie and Emmett lived in the early 1950s.

Mamie & Emmett Till home & Landmark, 6427 S. Lawrence Avenue

FLORENCE BEATRICE SMITH PRICE'S FORMER HOME
424 E. Pershing Road (iconic twentieth century photographs on building façade)

FLORENCE BEATRICE SMITH PRICE

April 9, 1887–June 3, 1953
Occupation: pianist, composer, educator

Florence Beatrice Smith Price was an internationally renowned composer. Born in Little Rock, Arkansas on April 9, 1887, she learned to play the piano from her mother, a music teacher. Smith Price's first recital was at age four. By age eleven, she was a published composer, and by age fourteen, the valedictorian of her high school class. She wrote her first commissioned work at age sixteen.

Smith Price enrolled in the New England Conservatory of Music in Boston when she turned fourteen, having presented herself as Mexican rather than Black to dodge discrimination and improve her chances of acceptance. In 1906, she graduated from the New England Conservatory with a bachelor's degree in music. At only twenty-three years old, she accepted a position as chair of the Music Department at Clark University, a historically Black institution in Atlanta, Georgia.

In 1912, Smith Price returned to Little Rock, Arkansas, where she married and had three children. She founded the Little Rock Club of Musicians after being refused admission to the all-white Arkansas Music Teachers Association. Smith Price and the Club of Musicians taught music to Black children at segregated schools. A lynching in their community drove the Price family to move to Chicago in 1927.

Smith Price experienced many professional successes in Chicago, where she studied at the American Conservatory of Music and the Chicago Musical College. She composed work that wove melody and rhythms of Black cultural significance and religious spirituality with European Romantic mood and technique. Smith Price also composed radio ads, worked as an organist for silent film screenings, and published songs for piano. One of her works, *Symphony in E Minor*, won first place in a 1932 competition for Black composers called the Wanamaker Prize. As a result, her work was performed by the Chicago Symphony Orchestra at the Chicago "Century of Progress" World's Fair in 1933; it was the first time a major orchestra had performed a symphony by a Black woman.

A pioneering classical composer, Smith Price continued to teach and compose until her 1953 death. She wrote over three hundred works, most of them unpublished, including chamber music, vocal compositions, and music for radio. Other notable compositions include her musical setting of Langston Hughes's "Song to the Dark Virgin" and *Concerto in One Movement.*

Additional landmarks and locations

Lived temporarily with Estella and **Margaret Allison Bonds** at 6652 S. Wabash Avenue.

Institutional affiliations

Negro Dance Art Studio

New England Conservatory of Music

Clark University

Chicago Symphony Orchestra

American Society of Composers, Authors and Publishers

Lincoln Memorial

R. Nathaniel Dett Club of Music and the Allied Arts

American Conservatory of Music

Chicago Teachers College

Central YMCA College

University of Chicago

Chicago Musical College (now Chicago College of Performing Arts of Roosevelt University)

Women's Symphony Orchestra of Chicago

WGN Radio

1933 Chicago World's Fair

Holstein Prize (*Opportunity* magazine)

IDA B. WELLS HOMES LANDMARK
3701 S. King Drive

The Ida B. Wells homes were built in Bronzeville as a part of the Chicago Housing Authority's public housing projects from 1939 to 1941. The homes were created under the "Neighborhood Composition Rule," a federal policy that upheld segregation by requiring that residents of a housing project be the same race as the majority of people in the neighborhood where the project would be located. At the project's height, there were over sixteen hundred African American families living in the units as the South Side's population drastically increased during the Great Migration.

Named after journalist, antilynching activist, suffragist, and clubwoman **Ida Bell Wells-Barnett**, the homes spanned three blocks and included a city park. They remained in Bronzeville for over sixty years, until the Chicago Housing Authority tore down the buildings between the years 2002 and 2011. In 2021, a historical marker was erected in the empty field where the homes had stood to honor the legacy of Ida Bell Wells-Barnett and the housing project that had been home to so many. The marker sits atop a large rock at the corner of E. 37th Street and South King Drive.

LEANITA MCCLAIN

October 2, 1951–May 28, 1984
Occupation: journalist, writer, commentator

Leanita McClain was born and raised on Chicago's South Side. She was the youngest daughter of Elizabeth and Lloyd McClain, who lived in Bronzeville's Ida B. Wells public housing project. Upon graduating from Northwestern University, McClain was offered a position as general assignment reporter for the *Chicago Tribune*.

She quickly excelled in her career, receiving multiple promotions. McClain was the second Black person in the position of *Tribune* staff columnist and became the highest-ranking Black woman in the paper's history at the time. While working at the *Tribune*, McClain met Clarence Page. The two wed in 1974 and were married for eight years.

McClain was the recipient of numerous awards, featured on the ABC talk show *Nightline*, and published nationally in *Newsweek* magazine, the *Washington Post*, and *Chicago Magazine*. She also shared her skills with young people by teaching a journalism course at Howard University.

Often, McClain expressed unpopular opinions in her columns. Some of her writings garnered international support, while others garnered hate mail. Her controversial reporting on the election of Chicago's first Black mayor, Harold Washington, generated racial backlash and death threats.

In private, McClain struggled with her mental health in ways that only her close friends and family knew about. Ultimately, she died by suicide at the age of thirty-two. After her tragic death, her former husband published a collection of McClain's essays which spanned her ten year career.

ALICE CROLLEY BROWNING'S HOME | 4019 S. Vincennes Avenue

ALICE CROLLEY BROWNING

November 5, 1907–October 15, 1985
Occupation: writer, publisher, editor

Alice Crolley Browning was born in 1907 at **Provident Hospital**. She graduated from Englewood High School and Chicago Normal School, receiving her bachelor's degree from the **University of Chicago** in 1931. She later worked toward a master's degree in English at Columbia University. Browning taught at Forrestville Elementary School in Bronzeville from 1935 to 1974. She was sixteen years old when she married sociologist George Franklin, with whom she had one daughter. In 1936, Browning married her second husband, Charles P. Browning, who would become vice president and director of advertising at the *Chicago Defender.*

Browning first made her name in the literary world as the founding editor of *Negro Story* magazine, which ran from 1944 to 1946. She started the magazine with her friend Fern Gayden, a social worker, in part as a response to the difficulties she had encountered trying to get her own writing published. Gayden, who had participated in Richard Wright's South Side Writers Group in the late 1930s, helped secure permission to reprint Wright's short story "Almos' a Man" in the magazine's May 1944 inaugural issue. The two women published the issue using $200 Browning borrowed from her husband. *Negro Story* went on to publish works by **Gwendolyn Brooks**, Ralph Ellison, Langston Hughes, Richard Wright, Chester Himes, **Margaret Taylor Goss Burroughs**, and Shirley Du Bois.

In 1970, Browning cofounded the

International Black Writers Conference, an important annual literary meeting that attracted writers including Gwendolyn Brooks, Alex Haley, Lerone Bennett, Margaret Walker Alexander, Oscar Brown Jr., Sam Greenlee, and Haki R. Madhubuti. Browning continued to be instrumental in the conference until 1984. She died the next year at Crestwood Nursing Home in Chicago.

NORA HOLT'S HOME | 4405 S. Prairie Avenue

NORA HOLT
November 1883–January 25, 1974
Occupation: music critic, composer, writer, editor

Born in Missouri, Nora Douglas Holt came to Chicago in 1915 to study music at Chicago Musical College. There, she obtained a bachelor's degree and was the first Black woman to earn her master's degree in music. Holt worked as the first music critic for the *Chicago Defender*. She was well known for her knowledge of classical music and passion for opera and symphony orchestra. During her time at the *Defender*, Holt gained a reputation for her meticulous assessments of musical performances and used her platform to amplify Black music.

Holt was active in the music community. Her home at 4405 S. Prairie Avenue was the birthplace of multiple music organizations, including the Chicago Music Association; *Music and Poetry*, a magazine that featured the work of important musicians throughout the nation; and the National Association of Negro Musicians, for which she served as vice president. Though short-lived, *Music and Poetry* was widely popular and recognized by local and national publications.

Throughout her career, Holt traveled internationally as a composer and writer. She eventually moved to New York City to become the music editor of the *New York Amsterdam News*. Holt took her passion for music to the airwaves in 1953 to host a radio program called *Nora Holt's Concert Showcase*.

Institutional affiliations

National Association
of Negro Musicians
Chicago Music Association
Chicago Defender
Phyllis Wheatley Home
Music Critics Circle of New York

EBENEZER MISSIONARY BAPTIST CHURCH
4501 S. Vincennes Avenue

The first congregation of Ebenezer Missionary Baptist Church was founded in 1902. During the Great Migration, hundreds of thousands of Black families traveled to Chicago to find both a geographical and a spiritual base. Many of them settled on the South Side and became a part of Ebenezer. The church is known as the birthplace of gospel music, which formed as the early congregations brought their Southern musical traditions to the Midwest.

ROBERTA EVELYN WINSTON MARTIN

February 14, 1906–January 13, 1969
Occupation: gospel music performer, pianist, singer, composer, writer, publisher, choir organizer

Roberta Evelyn Martin was born Lubirda Winston. She was originally from Arkansas but moved to Chicago with her parents as a child. Her music career began when she took on the role of pianist at **Ebenezer Missionary Baptist Church.** Martin was invited to join Ebenezer's junior gospel choir by choir director Theodore R. Frye and pianist Thomas A. Dorsey, both of whom went on to earn reputations as pioneers in the gospel genre.

Martin and Frye began a romantic relationship, and together started the gospel group the Martin-Frye Singers. When the relationship ended, Martin expanded and renamed the group the Roberta Martin Singers. She composed, arranged, and recorded songs that gained national popularity. In 1939, Martin opened the Roberta Martin Studio of Music. The gospel music scene in Chicago transitioned into an industry, and the company became one of the largest gospel publishers in the city.

Martin also maintained her own independent music career. Over the span of more than three decades, she created a lasting musical repertoire, publishing over 280 songs, many of which she arranged herself. She also received six gold records for selling one million or more copies of a single record or song. Over fifty thousand people came to her funeral, which was held at Mount Pisgah Baptist Church in Chicago.

Institutional affiliations

Roberta Martin Studio of Music
Mount Pisgah Baptist Church

LILLIAN "LIL" HARDIN ARMSTRONG'S HOME
421 E. 44th Street

LILLIAN "LIL" HARDIN ARMSTRONG 💼 🖌
February 3, 1898–August 27, 1971
Occupation: composer, pianist, band leader, musician

Born in Memphis on February 3, 1898, Lillian ("Lil") Hardin Armstrong was a prolific and pioneering jazz pianist and bandleader who composed more than 150 pieces of music in her lifetime. Armstrong began formally studying music when she was four years old. She later studied music at Fisk University, but never completed her program of study there, instead joining her mother to live in Chicago in 1918. She worked at Jones Music Store at 3409 S. State Street as a "demonstrator" who played sheet music for customers. After that, Armstrong was hired by the New Orleans Creole Jazz

Band and played in clubs across Chicago, before briefly touring across the country as a member of King Oliver's jazz band.

When Louis Armstrong was hired by the Oliver band to play the cornet and the second trumpet, he and Lil met and began dating. They were married in February 1924, a second marriage for both. Lil encouraged Louis to leave the Oliver band and become a soloist.

Together, the two of them wrote numerous jazz compositions, and much of Louis's success can be traced to his wife's contributions and influence. Lil was a member of Louis's Hot Five.

In 1925, the Armstrongs bought a home at 421 E. 44th Street. As Louis's fame and success grew, the Armstrongs' marriage began to fail, and they divorced in 1938. Lil took her ex-husband to court for copyright control of the songs she'd written and/or co-composed. She continued to work and create music after the divorce, leading two all-women jazz groups and a co-ed group in the 1930s. She also became a house pianist for Decca Recording Company. One of her compositions, titled "Just for a Thrill," was a major hit for Ray Charles.

In August 1971, the seventy-three-year-old Armstrong went to New York to play piano for a televised memorial to Louis, who had died in early July. Lil died onstage after suffering a massive heart attack.

Additional landmarks and locations

Lillian Hardin Armstrong Park, 4433 S. St. Lawrence Avenue

More to read

Just for a Thrill: Lil Hardin, First Lady of Jazz by James L. Dickerson (Cooper Square Press, 2002)

Born to Swing: Lil Hardin Armstrong's Life in Jazz by Mara Rockliff and Michele Wood (Calkins Creek Press, 2018)

DUSABLE HIGH SCHOOL | 4934 S. Wabash Street; 24 E. 50th Street

ADDIE LORAINE WYATT

March 8, 1924-March 28, 2012
Occupation: labor and civil rights
activist and leader, minister

Addie Loraine Wyatt was born as Addie Cameron in Mississippi in 1924. In 1930, she moved to Chicago with her mother and siblings to join her father, who had fled Mississippi after an altercation with his white boss. Growing up very poor, Wyatt moved locations often, but her family eventually settled at 4243 S. Calumet Avenue. Wyatt grew up very religious; she and her family were parishioners of Langley Avenue Church of God, located at 4338 S. Prairie Avenue. She started attending **DuSable High School** in 1936, at the age of twelve. There, she met Claude S. Wyatt, whom she married at the age of sixteen. After Addie's mother died in 1940, she and Claude took on responsibility for her six younger siblings. Her father's alcoholism and her older brother's service in the military made them unable to care for the children. Needing money to supplement her husband's salary, Wyatt applied for a job as a typist for Armour and Company. However, she was sent to the canning department because Black women were not hired as typists.

In adulthood, Wyatt was active in union politics. She was elected an officer of her union, Local 56 of the United Packinghouse Workers of America (UPWA), in 1953, becoming the first Black female officer of the branch. In the 1970s, she was instrumental in the founding of the Coalition of Black Trade Unionists and the Coalition of Labor Union Women (CLUW). In 1976, she became the first woman elected to serve on the executive board–as an international vice president–of the Amalgamated Meat Cutters and Butcher Workmen of North America.

As an ordained minister, Wyatt and Claude established the Vernon Park Church of God in 1955. The couple raised funds for Martin Luther King Jr.'s social justice work and participated in some of the major civil rights marches of the 1960s. Wyatt also fought energetically for women's rights, assisting in laying the foundation for the National Organization for Women (NOW) in 1966. Earlier in that decade, she had been selected by Eleanor Roosevelt to serve on the President's Commission on the Status of Women. Wyatt was a prominent advocate for the Equal Rights Amendment and served as the national vice president of the National Council of Negro Women.

In 1975, *TIME* named Wyatt one of the "Twelve Women of the Year." Over the years, she received many awards for her contributions to organized labor, and went onto provide mentorship to a young Barack Obama when he worked in Chicago community organizing.

Additional landmarks and locations

Altgeld Gardens

Addie Wyatt Childhood home, 4934 S. Wabash Avenue

Institutional affiliations

United Packinghouse Workers of America

Coordinating Council for Community Organizations

Southern Christian Leadership Conference

Chicago Freedom Movement

Operation Breadbasket

More to read

Reverend Addie Wyatt: Faith and the Fight for Labor, Gender, and Racial Equality by Marcia Walker-McWilliams (University of Illinois Press, 2016)

CLARICE DURHAM

November 12, 1919–April 20, 2018
Occupation: community organizer, political activist, educator

Born in Mobile, Alabama, on November 12, 1919, Clarice Durham grew up in Chattanooga, Tennessee. At the age of eleven, Durham and her siblings migrated to Chicago to live with their maternal grandfather after the death of their parents.

One of the first causes Durham supported was bringing awareness to inequality under the law in the infamous Scottsboro case. Nine Black boys from Alabama were wrongfully accused of raping two white women on a train and sentenced to death in 1931. Durham circulated information about the Scottsboro case to locals in Chicago and advocated for their freedom. As a teenager, she admired a communist group that met in her neighborhood at Ellis Park. The group

worked to rehouse and protect people who had recently been evicted.

In 1937, Durham graduated as the valedictorian of her **DuSable High School** senior class. As a young adult, she earned a bachelor's degree from Pestalozzi-Froebel Teachers College and a master's degree from Roosevelt University. She also studied at the **University of Chicago** and Northwestern University. Her professional work was in education, teaching kindergarten and Head Start for Chicago Public Schools (CPS). By the time she retired in 1990, Durham was the district coordinator of Head Start.

Throughout her life, Durham

fought for desegregation. While teaching for CPS, she supported the successful boycott of the crowded and poorly resourced "Willis wagons" used throughout the 1950s and 1960s to prevent Black students from integrating into white, segregated schools. Durham also pursued desegregation work at the national level through the Progressive Party of 1948, which she helped form. She was a chair of the Chicago Alliance Against Racist and Political Repression and served as treasurer of the Chicago branch of the National Anti-Imperialist Movement in Solidarity with African Liberation (NAIMSAL). In 1963, she participated in the March on Washington and was active in Harold Washington's Chicago mayoral campaign.

Durham was also an arts patron and editor of the weekly *Destination Freedom* radio series, which dramatized the lives of African American heroes.

Institutional affiliations

Pestalozzi-Froebel Teachers College
Roosevelt University
NAACP
National Anti-Imperialist Movement in Solidarity with African Liberation
African National Congress
Teachers for Quality Education
Chicago Public Schools
Chicago Alliance Against Racist and Political Repression
Destination Freedom
Vivian G. Harsh Research Collection
University of Chicago
Northwestern University
Harold Washington mayoral campaign
Student Woodlawn Area Project

Additional landmarks and locations

Doolittle Elementary School
Wendell Phillips Elementary School
Ellis Park
Former home,
2625 S. Michigan Avenue

MAHALIA JACKSON'S FORMER RESIDENCE
5100 S. Cornell Avenue

MAHALIA JACKSON

October 26, 1911–January 27, 1972
Occupation: singer, performer,
civil rights activist

Mahalia Jackson is remembered as the "Queen of Gospel." Born in New Orleans, she migrated to Chicago in late 1927, when she was seventeen, hoping to become a nurse. Shortly after her arrival, she joined the Greater Salem Baptist Church (then located at 30th Street and LaSalle Street, now located at 215 W. 71st Street). Jackson sang in its choir. She made her living working as a laundress and then as a beautician. Jackson struck up a friendship with Thomas A. Dorsey, a legendary gospel composer, musician, and Baptist minister, who began to write songs for her.

Jackson began recording music in 1937. Her recording of "Move On Up a Little Higher" (1946) sold nearly two million copies and introduced gospel music to larger, mainstream audiences. By 1950, she was an established performer, singing at Carnegie Hall and completing several European tours. By 1954, Jackson had her own TV show.

In 1956, when Jackson bought her home in an all-white community at 8358 S. Indiana Avenue, people verbally and physically harassed her, including firing bullets through her living room window. However, Jackson refused to be intimidated and did not move. She condemned housing discrimination when she appeared on Edward R. Murrow's *Person to Person* show in 1958.

At the request of her friend Martin Luther King Jr., Jackson sang at the 1963 March on Washington. She also sang King's favorite song, "Take My Hand, Precious Lord," at his funeral in 1968. She died of heart failure in 1972.

Institutional affiliations

Greater Salem Baptist Church

Additional landmarks and locations

Jackson performed at **Ebenezer Missionary Baptist Church** at 4501 S. Vincennes Avenue.

Mahalia Jackson Park is located at 8385 S. Bickhoff Avenue, a few blocks away from the home she purchased in 1956 (at 8358 S. Indiana Avenue).

HYDE PARK HIGH SCHOOL
6220 S. Stony Island Avenue

DIANE NASH 🏢 ⛫
May 15, 1938–
Occupation: civil rights activist,
strategist, educator

Civil rights activist Diane Nash was born in Chicago on May 15, 1938. A devout Catholic, Nash initially thought that she would become a nun. She first became actively involved with the student wing of the civil rights movement in 1959, when she enrolled at Fisk University in Nashville, Tennessee and came face-to-face with the pervasive segregation of the Jim Crow South for the first time in her life. Her determination and courage, coupled with her "flawless instincts," quickly made her one of the most respected strategists and leaders of the sit-in movement in Nashville.

Nash's early efforts included orchestrating the first successful civil rights campaign to desegregate lunch counters and being a founding member of the Student Nonviolent Coordinating Committee, or SNCC. SNCC became one of the most influential groups during the civil rights movement of the fifties and sixties. After marrying civil rights activist James Bevel in 1961, she moved to Jackson,

Mississippi, where she began organizing voter registration and school desegregation campaigns for the Southern Christian Leadership Conference (SCLC). Nash and Bevel received the SCLC's Rosa Parks Award from Martin Luther King Jr. in 1965. Their work with the Selma right-to-vote movement paved the way for the Voting Rights Act of 1965.

President John F. Kennedy appointed Nash to a national committee for the passage of the Civil Rights Act of 1964. She continued working with the SCLC until 1965, serving as an organizer, strategist, and field and race-relations staff person. Nash later questioned the dominance of men, especially clergymen, in the SCLC, and called for the inclusion and active participation of women.

Nash currently resides in Chicago, where she works in fair housing advocacy and real estate, and as an educator and lecturer.

MINNIE RIPERTON
November 8, 1947–July 12, 1979
Occupation: singer, songwriter,
women's health advocate

Minnie Riperton was born on November 8, 1947, on the South Side of Chicago. She was exposed to music through her family at an early age; her mother, Thelma, registered a ten-year-old Minnie for music classes at the **Abraham Lincoln Center**. Riperton aspired to become an opera singer, but later developed an interest in rock-n-roll and rhythm-and-blues music.

In 1963, Raynard Miner and Rose Miller discovered Riperton as she was performing at **Hyde Park High School**. They recruited her to sing with a local girls' singing group called The Gems. Riperton recorded songs at Chicago's renowned Chess Records while also working at the company as a receptionist. She is best known for her 1975 number one hit, "Loving You." After Riperton was diagnosed with breast cancer in 1976, she became an advocate for women's health. Tragically, she died of her illness in 1979, at the age of 31.

Additional landmarks and locations

Riperton's childhood home is located at 546 E. Oakwood Boulevard.

Riperton also lived at 608 E. Oakwood Boulevard for a time.

UNIVERSITY OF CHICAGO
1131 E. 57th Street

KATERINE DUNHAM
KATHERINE DUNHAM

June 22, 1909-May 21, 2006
Occupation: anthropologist, dancer,
choreographer, teacher

Katherine Dunham was born in Chicago on June 22, 1909. An activist, writer, social anthropologist, and highly trained dancer, she is often called the "matriarch" of Black dance and considered an ancestor in African American dance communities. At the age of twenty-one, she created Ballet Nègre, one of the first Black ballet companies in the United States. In 1934, Dunham's company performed at the Chicago World's Fair; the following year, Dunham received her degree in social anthropology from the **University of Chicago**. In 1937, she was offered the position of dance director for Chicago's Negro Unit of the Federal Theatre Project.

Dunham used various art forms to express African American and African diasporic narratives. According to Joanna Dee Das, "She wove together ballet, modern dance, Afro-Caribbean forms, African American vernacular traditions, and Asian movement vocabularies in her choreography, challenging high/low, modern/ethnic cultural hierarchies." Dunham's choreography explored the intersections of capitalism, imperialism, and global racism. With her work, she actively sought to avoid reproducing stereotypes while celebrating the liberatory power of performance.

Dunham built institutions as a way of combating cultural erasure. She established the short-lived Negro Dance Group in Chicago's Hyde Park in the early 1930s. In 1944, she built the Katherine Dunham School of Dance in Manhattan's theater district. Her students included Marlon Brando, Arthur Mitchell, and James Dean. In 1967, she opened the Performing Arts Training Center in East St. Louis.

Institutional affiliations

NAACP

Urban League

Katherine Dunham School of Arts and Research

Festival of Black Arts in Dakar, Senegal

Additional landmarks and locations

The Negro Dance Group school was in Hyde Park's artists' colony at 57th Street and Stony Island Avenue. No trace of the art colony remains today.

More to read

A Touch of Innocence: A Memoir of Childhood by Katherine Dunham (The University of Chicago Press, 1994)

Katherine Dunham: Dance and the African Diaspora by Joanna Dee Das (Oxford University Press, 2017)

MARGARET ALLISON BONDS'S CHILDHOOD HOME
6652 S. Wabash Avenue

MARGARET ALLISON BONDS

March 2, 1913–April 26, 1972
Occupation: composer, pianist, educator, editor

A child progidy, Margaret Allison Bonds became one of the most influential composers and pianists of the twentieth century. Bonds was born and raised in Chicago, with music at the center of her life. Her mother, Estella C. Bonds, was a well-known organist, pianist, and music educator and founding member of the National

Association of Negro Musicians (NANM). Her mother taught Bonds how to play the piano at such an early age that by the time she was five years old, she had already composed her first song and received a scholarship to study at the Coleridge-Taylor School of Music.

Bonds grew up encountering prominent African American artists who frequented her home, including singer Abbie Mitchell, composer Noble Sissle, and poet Countee Cullen. Before she turned ten, she had won two scholarships from the Chicago Musical College. She studied under notable musicians in the Chicago community, including pianist and composer **Florence Beatrice Smith Price**, who mentored Bonds and shared a decades-long friendship with her.

Bonds' talents continued to advance rapidly. She attended Northwestern University when she was only sixteen years old. Due to the racism and segregation of the early 1900s, Bonds was not allowed to stay in the designated student housing and was forced to commute to campus. After graduating with a bachelor's degree in music in 1933, she received a fellowship to support her graduate studies, and she received her master's degree one year later.

In 1933, Bonds participated in the Chicago World's Fair as the first African American featured soloist with the Chicago Symphony Orchestra. During the same concert, the orchestra performed a work by Price, becoming the first major American orchestra to perform a symphony by a Black woman composer.

In the late 1930s, Bonds founded the Allied Arts Academy, a school on the South Side of Chicago where she served as director and taught piano and composition. After the school closed, she decided to pursue her artistic dreams in New York City. There, Bonds became an editor for a music publishing company and attended classes at the Juilliard School of Music.

During her time in New York, Bonds also created the Margaret Bonds Chamber Society to support the work of Black composers and musicians and helped to establish the Harlem Cultural Community Center. She served as music director for multiple New York City theaters and toured as both a soloist and part of a piano duo.

Bonds was close friends with Langston Hughes, and the two collaborated on various projects throughout her career. In 1940, she married Lawrence Richardson, a probation officer. The couple had one daughter together.

Bonds left behind a legacy of over ninety compositions in several genres, including theater, film, spiritual, pop, and jazz. Many of her songs became national and international hits.

Institutional affiliations

National Association
of Negro Musicians

Chicago Music Association

American Society of Composers,
Authors and Publishers

Harlem Cultural Community Center

East Side Settlement House

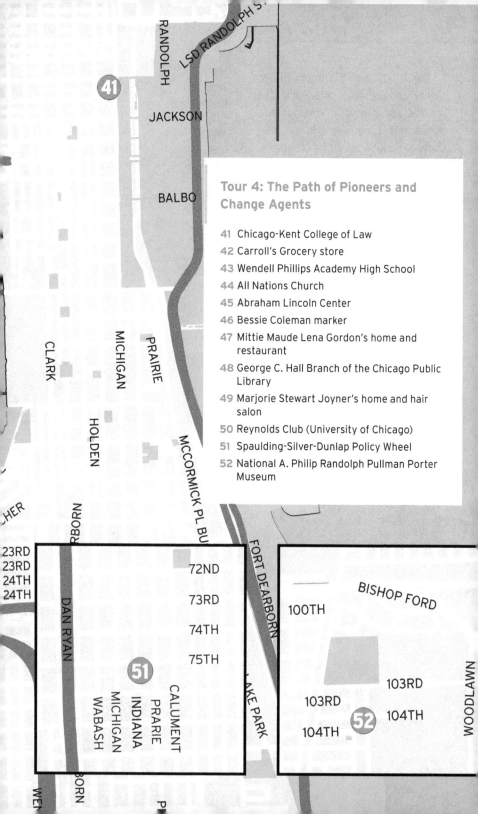

Tour 4: The Path of Pioneers and Change Agents

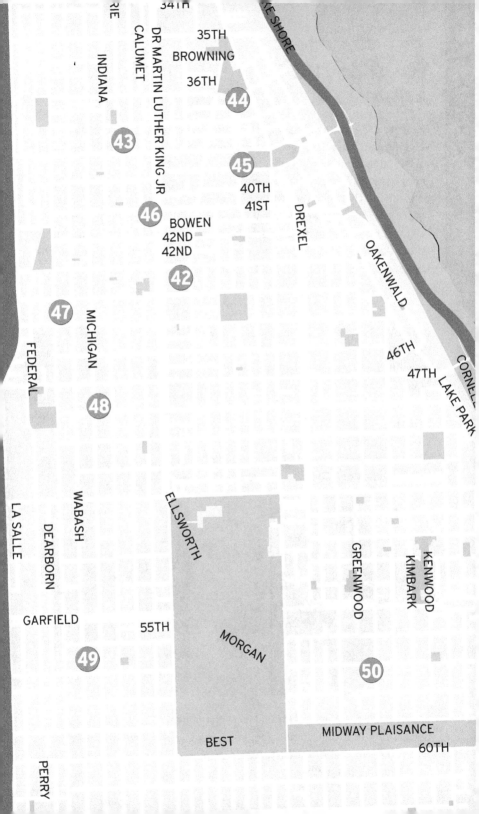

TOUR 4: THE PATH OF PIONEERS AND CHANGE AGENTS

Pioneers are agents of change. They are the women setting precedents, developing pathways through organizations, and inventing intellectual structures and tools that would elevate local policy, culture, and industry. Many of them were the "first," their accomplishments expanding possibilities for the generations that followed. Others were leaders in refusing to be held back by economic, social, and political obstacles. Although many of their names are not a part of mainstream narratives, the women featured in this tour are influential changemakers and legendary icons within their fields who challenged the status quo and forged new paths.

CHICAGO-KENT COLLEGE OF LAW
116 S. Michigan Avenue (now the Lake View Building, formerly the Municipal Courts Building)

SOPHIA BELL BOAZ 💼
Lifespan Dates: unknown
Occupation: lawyer, social worker, probation officer at the Cook County Juvenile Court

Sophia Bell Boaz graduated from Fisk University in Nashville, Tennessee, in 1911, after which she moved to Chicago and lived in the Charles Sumner Settlement at 31 W. Lake Street. At the time, social workers would live in settlement houses and become part of the communities they served.

Two years later, Boaz was appointed a Cook County probation officer. She contributed to a research study titled "The Colored People of Chicago: An Investigation Made for the Juvenile Protective Association," which was the first of its kind. The study contained statistical information on the welfare of Black people of all ages and statuses in the city, including their housing, education, opportunities for employment, and available resources.

Boaz graduated from **Chicago-Kent College of Law** in 1922 and was admitted to the bar in 1923. She continued in her civil rights efforts by maintaining a staff position in the city's juvenile and domestic relations courts, offering her services in a way that resembled a social work agency. In 1943, she was one of the first three Black women admitted to the National Association of Women Lawyers.

When Sophia Bell Boaz attended **Chicago-Kent College of Law**, it was in the Municipal Courts Building (also known as the Lake View Building) at 116 S. Michigan Avenue. The law school remained at that site from 1924 until 1976, when it moved to 10-12 N. Franklin Street.

CARROLL'S GROCERY STORE
457 E. 43rd Street

Cora Carroll's store has been demolished; the field where it was once located is all that remains.

CORA CARROLL 🏛️ 💡
Lifespan Dates: unknown
Occupation: businesswoman, entrepreneur, community leader, activist

Cora Carroll was elected the "Mayor of Bronzeville" in 1959 and was the first woman to hold the office. This ceremonial position was first created by the *Chicago Defender* in 1932. Votes for the honor were tallied by mail and numbered in the tens of millions. Carroll won her first election with nearly twelve million votes and served a second term after being reelected in 1961. During the 1970s, Carroll also served in a similar honorary position as vice mayor of "Defenderland."

Originally from Mississippi, Carroll owned and operated **Carroll's Grocery Store** at 457 E. 43rd Street with her husband. In her honorary capacity, she organized events and civic participation. Carroll served in various other positions, including chairing the 43rd Street unit of the Cosmopolitan Chamber of Commerce. In this capacity, she organized neighbors in 1969 to stop the demolition of the *Wall of Respect*, an effort that succeeded until 1972.

WENDELL PHILLIPS ACADEMY HIGH SCHOOL
244 E. Pershing Road

Designed by architect William Bryce Mundie in 1904, Wendell Phillips Academy High School was initially racially integrated. In its early history, the student body was predominantly white and wealthy. As the community's makeup changed, so did the composition of the student body. According to the city of Chicago, by the early 1920s, Phillips had become the city's first predominantly Black high school. In 2003, it was designated as a Chicago landmark. Notable alumni include Nat King Cole, Irene McCoy, Sam Cooke, and John H. Johnson.

MAUDELLE TANNER BROWN BOUSFIELD

June 1, 1885–October 14, 1971
Occupation: educator, principal,
researcher, education activist

Maudelle Tanner Brown Bousfield's legacy is built on a lifetime commitment to education, starting as a teacher and moving into administration. Born in St. Louis, Bousfield was the first Black person to be appointed dean of girls at **Wendell Phillips Academy High School** and later became the first Black principal of the school. She was also the first Black principal of Chicago's Keith Elementary School and served as principal of Stephen A. Douglas Elementary School.

As the population of Black children increased during the Great Migration, overcrowding became a major problem, and standardized testing emerged as a leading measure of youth intelligence. Bousfield researched the disproportionate impact of these two phenomena on Black children. She advocated for unbiased alternatives and for integrated schools where Black students could be taught in adequate learning environments. Bousfield also called for a comprehensive overhaul in all areas of study for Black children, with an emphasis on history and teacher training. Her research, some of which was published in the *Journal of Negro Education*, highlighted the economic inequalities that caused Black children to be at a social disadvantage throughout their

Bousfield, left, with the other founding members of the Women's Policy Committee of the War Manpower Commission, 1942

lives, starting with how they are educated in classrooms.

In 1906, Bousfield became the first Black woman to graduate from the University of Illinois, and she later earned a master's degree from the **University of Chicago** Graduate School. She was one of the first Black people on the Board of Oral Examiners of Chicago and was also a member of the Women's Advisory Committee of the War Manpower Commission and the Advisory Committee of the Mississippi Health Project.

Institutional affiliations

Wendell Phillips Academy High School
University of Illinois
Keith Elementary School
Mississippi Health Project
Mendelssohn Conservatory of Music
Chicago Defender
Stephen A. Douglass
Elementary School
Coolidge School

IRENE MCCOY GAINES

October 25, 1892-April 7, 1964
Occupation: political organizer,
civil rights activist, clubwoman

Irene McCoy Gaines was a graduate of the **Wendell Phillips Academy High School**. Gaines went on to become a renowned Chicago community leader and civil rights activist. Her life's work was anchored in organizing Black women in the political realm and providing support for children.

Born in Ocala, Florida, in 1892, Gaines was moved to Chicago in infancy. She attended college at Fisk University and came back to Chicago after graduation. A Black clubwoman, she foregrounded women's rights in her organizing career. She worked as a stenographer until World War I opened opportunities for her to move into full-time social work. Gaines held a variety of positions in the field within organizations including the Cook County Bureau of Public Welfare, the Juvenile Court, the **Cook County Hospital**, the Veterans Bureau, and the YWCA.

Gaines fought to improve educational access for pregnant teenagers and helped to develop one of Chicago's first integrated nursery schools. Additionally, she organized support and training for Black domestic workers. As founder and president of the Chicago Council of Negro Organizations, Gaines organized a group to advocate for workers' rights, brought attention to housing discrimination, and pushed for fair employment practices among labor unions and businesses throughout the nation.

Gaines took part in organizing the Illinois Federation of Republican Colored Women's Clubs and became its president in 1924. She also became a part of the Northern District Federation of Colored Women's Clubs and served as its secretary. Moving further into the political realm, she became one of the first Black women to run for the Illinois state legislature. She was also the first Black woman to run for the Chicago Board of County Commissioners—running on the Republican ticket in 1950. Gaines lost both elections.

Institutional affiliations

Congress of American Women

National Association of Colored Women's Clubs

Chicago Council of Negro Organizations

Illinois Federation of Republican Colored Women's Clubs

War Camp Community Service

Chicago Women's Trade Union League

Chicago Northern District Federation of Colored Women's Clubs

League of Women Voters

YWCA

Additional landmarks and locations

Gaines's home was located at 3262 S. Vernon Avenue; housing in this area was demolished to build the Lake Meadows housing project.

MADELINE ROBINSON MORGAN STRATTON MORRIS 🏢 🐚 ⚒

August 14, 1906–December 26, 2007
Occupation: teacher, education activist

Madeline Robinson Morgan Stratton Morris was a lifelong teacher and education activist known for developing the first Black history curriculum used by a major US city's public school system. She was born in Chicago and earned an elementary school teaching certificate from Chicago Teachers College in 1929, before starting work at Emerson Elementary School in 1933. She later obtained a bachelor's degree and master's degree in education from Northwestern University, completing additional graduate work at the **University of Chicago.**

In 1941, Morris began developing the "Supplementary Units for a Course in Social Studies" to highlight Black experiences in US history classrooms. Chicago became the first major US city to adopt such a curriculum, and the "Supplementary Units" for grades one through eight were taught in Chicago Public Schools between 1942 and 1945. Morris believed that the knowledge of Black history would encourage Black students to succeed and combat anti-Black racism. It was this work that catapulted her into leadership of the movement to develop and teach Black history. Her work was immediately recognized nationally and internationally by civic organizations, educational institutions, and school boards looking to have African American history curricula implemented in their institutions.

Morris taught at Chicago Public Schools for thirty-five years, retiring in 1968, and published several books on education and the Black experience, including *Strides Forward: Afro-American Biographies and Negroes Who Helped Build America.* She has been honored by the National Council of Negro Women and the National Negro Museum and Historical Foundation. Her personal papers were donated to the Vivian G. Harsh Research collection of Afro-American History and Literature at the Carter G. Woodson Branch of the Chicago Public Library. She died in Chicago in 2007.

Institutional affiliations

Human Relations Committee of the Chicago Board of Education
National Council of Negro Women
Association for the Study of Negro Life and History
Chicago Teachers College
Emerson Elementary School
Northwestern University
University of Chicago
Mayfair College
Chicago State University
Governors State University
National Negro Museum and Historical Foundation
Sigma Gamma Rho Sorority

Additional landmarks and locations

Morris was contracted at:

Emerson Elementary School

Farren Elementary School

Englewood High School

Drake Elementary School

A. O. Sexton Elementary School

Dixon Elementary School

Wendell Phillips Academy High School

ALL NATIONS CHURCH | 3716 S. Langley Avenue

The original All Nations Church has since been demolished; a field remains in its place.

LUCINDA "LUCY" MADDEN SMITH

January 14, 1875–June 18, 1952
Occupation: minister, faith healer,
community leader

Lucinda Madden Smith was born in Woodstock, Georgia, in 1875. In 1910, she and her nine children moved to Chicago after her husband, William Smith, abandoned the family. Smith later rejoined his family and remained with them until his 1938 death.

"Lucy" Smith established the Langley Avenue All Nations Pentecostal Church in 1918, first as an outdoor traveling church with no set home-base. In 1926, All Nations began to congregate at a building at 3716 S. Langley Avenue. It was the first Chicago church ever established by a woman pastor, and the first major Chicago congregation led by a Black woman pastor. Women took on almost all the leadership roles in the church, in contrast with more traditional Black churches in Chicago. By the mid-1930s, the church boasted a membership of over five thousand parishioners. Smith helped shape religious culture in Chicago by providing social services and support. Specifically, her church addressed critical food and clothing needs, providing both resources to thousands of Chicagoans during the Great Depression.

Known as Elder Lucy Smith, Smith was also a pioneer of gospel radio. All Nations was renowned for its music, and in 1933 Smith started a radio program to disseminate sermons and performances more widely. The popular program—titled the *Glorious Church of the Air*—was the first live worship radio broadcast from a Black church, and it continued until 1955.

Smith's church was interracial, and people would come from across Chicago to attend. She considered herself a "faith healer" who could cure various ailments with her touch.

When Elder Lucy Smith died in 1952, the *Chicago Defender* called her funeral "the largest funeral in Chicago history." Her body lay in state at three locations: her home at 3810 S. Parkway (now King Drive); A.A. Rayner's Chapel; and All Nations. **Mahalia Jackson** sang at her funeral, and four hundred police officers were present, supposedly for the purpose of maintaining order at the funeral home. There were estimated to be over sixty thousand mourners and fifty thousand people who watched the funeral procession. Smith is buried in Lincoln Cemetery.

Additional landmarks and locations

Elder Lucy Madden Smith's home, 3810 S. King Drive

More to read

Passionately Human, No Less Divine: Religion and Culture in Black Chicago 1915-1952 by Wallace Best (Princeton University Press, 2005)

ABRAHAM LINCOLN CENTER | 700 E. Oakwood Boulevard

THYRA EDWARDS
December 25, 1897–July 9, 1953
Occupation: social worker, teacher, writer,
journalist, labor organizer, international activist

Thyra Edwards spent much of her life fighting to bring about political, social, and economic change for local, national, and global communities. Born in 1897 in Wharton, Texas, Edwards started her career as a teacher, later becoming a caseworker for the Joint Emergency Relief Commission and Illinois Emergency Relief Commission. She was also a journalist. Edwards worked to combat disparities in health, housing, and working conditions facing Black communities. During the 1930s, Edwards worked for the **Abraham Lincoln Center**, an interracial settlement house founded in 1905, to expand employment opportunities for African Americans, and took on a leadership position within the National Negro Congress.

Traveling as a foreign correspondent, Edwards wrote for several publications, including the *Chicago Defender*, *The Crisis* magazine, the *Pittsburgh Courier*, and *Woman Today*, a publication in the Soviet Union. Edwards used her writing platforms to bring attention to the parallels of discrimination, displacement, and poverty experienced by African Americans in the United States and minorities abroad. She also wrote extensively about the rise of fascism in Italy, Spain, and Germany.

Edwards often centered women and children in both her activism and her reporting. She was one of the first directors of the Lake County Children's Home for Black Orphans. Concerning international conditions, Edwards wrote about the lives of women and children in the Soviet Union and organized the first Jewish childcare program in Rome to assist children of the Holocaust.

Institutional affiliations

Lake County Children's Home
Brotherhood of Sleeping Car Porters
People's Voice newspaper
Associated Negro Press
Chicago School of Civics and Philanthropy (later the School of Social Service Administration at the University of Chicago)
National Negro Congress
Chicago Defender
Indiana University
National Negro Stop Hitler and Hitlerism Committee
Chicago Venereal Disease Control Program
Brookwood Labor College

Additional landmarks and locations

Chicago-Kent College of Law
University of Chicago

BESSIE COLEMAN MARKER
4101 S. King Drive

BESSIE COLEMAN
January 20, 1892-April 30, 1926
Occupation: pilot, aerial performer

Bessie Coleman was the first African American pilot. She was born in Texas and came to Chicago in 1910 as part of the Great Migration. Coleman worked as a manicurist at the White Sox Barber Shop; later, she was able to open a small chili parlor on 35th Street and Indiana Avenue. She lived with her family at 41st Street and South Park Avenue (now King Drive).

After learning that female pilots flew during World War I, Coleman decided to pursue a pilot's license. After being turned down by flying schools in the United States, many of which were operating under Jim Crow laws, the aspiring pilot decided to attend flight school in France. With financial support from Chicago entrepreneurs Robert S. Abbott and Jessie Binga, Coleman achieved her dream. After her training, she was granted an aviation license from the Fédération Aéronautique Internationale.

When Coleman returned to Chicago as the first licensed African American pilot, there were few opportunities available to her. It wasn't long before she set her sights on a new goal: opening her own aviation school to train Black pilots. To raise money to start the school, she became a barnstormer—a pilot who performed stunts as entertainment for large audiences. She garnered international recognition and toured the country giving lectures and performing in air shows. Coleman refused to fly before segregated audiences.

In 1926, Coleman died in a plane crash. As an annual tribute, Tuskegee Airmen and other Black pilots fly over Lincoln Cemetery and drop flowers on her grave to honor her legacy.

Institutional affiliations

Fédération Aéronautique Internationale

Additional landmarks and locations

Bessie Coleman Park,
5445 S. Drexel Avenue

Bessie Coleman Branch Library,
731 E. 63rd Street

MITTIE MAUDE LENA GORDON'S HOME AND RESTAURANT
4451 S. State Street

The home and restaurant has since been demolished; an empty field remains.

MITTIE MAUDE LENA GORDON

August 2, 1889– June 16, 1961
Occupation: movement leader, organizer

Born in Louisiana and raised in Arkansas, Mittie Maude Lena Gordon was a Black nationalist and former member of the Universal Negro Improvement Association. She founded the Peace Movement of Ethiopia in 1932.

The Peace Movement grew into the largest Black nationalist organization established by a woman in the United States, with about 300,000 members in Chicago and across the country. Many members of the movement were women who found opportunities to develop their leadership in the organization.

Gordon was staunchly pro-emigration to West Africa. In 1933, from her home in the Black Belt, which also doubled as a restaurant and meeting space, she launched an emigration campaign to Liberia. Gordon mailed a petition to President Franklin Roosevelt after collecting over 400,000 signatures from Black Americans willing to leave the United States to improve their circumstances. She asked for federal support for this relocation, but it never came.

Gordon was eventually put under surveillance by the FBI for her associations with Japanese politicians and organizations. In 1942, she was arrested for "conspiring with the Japanese" and jailed. Gordon was convicted and sentenced to two years in prison.

GEORGE C. HALL BRANCH OF THE CHICAGO PUBLIC LIBRARY | 4801 S. Michigan Avenue

VIVIAN GORDON HARSH 🏠 🏢 📚 🤝
May 27, 1890–August 17, 1960
Occupation: librarian, curator, historian

Born in Chicago on May 27, 1890, Vivian Gordon Harsh was a librarian devoted to African American studies. She graduated from **Wendell Phillips Academy High School** in 1908. In 1921, she received a degree from Simmons College Library School in Boston. Years later, she went on to take additional courses at the **University of Chicago** School of Library Science.

Along with other South Siders, Harsh pushed for a full-service library branch in Bronzeville. Sears magnate and philanthropist Julius Rosenwald, who agreed to help finance the new library, awarded Harsh a traveling scholarship as part of the effort. When the new George Cleveland Hall branch opened in 1932, Harsh became its first director and the first African American to head a branch of the Chicago Public Library. She organized literary clubs for reading texts by Black authors, and in 1934 she launched a public lecture series that featured writers and artists Zora Neale Hurston, **Gwendolyn Brooks**, and Langston Hughes. Harsh was joined by children's librarian **Charlemae Hill Rollins** in developing many community programs, including storytelling sessions, book and drama clubs, a Negro history club, and a series of "appreciation hours" that underscored Black contributions to literature and the arts.

Harsh began collecting materials related to African American history, often using her own money to cover the costs. Today, the Vivian G. Harsh Research Collection of Afro-American History and Literature is housed at the Carter G. Woodson Regional Library. The collection includes more than 70,000 books and other materials.

Institutional affiliations

Association for the Study of Negro Life and History

Parkway Community House

YWCA

NAACP

Sixth Grace Presbyterian Church

Additional landmarks and locations

Harsh Park (located at 4458–4470 S. Oakenwald Avenue, close to Harsh's childhood home)

Carter G. Woodson Regional Library's Vivian G. Harsh Research Collection of Afro-American History and Literature

CHARLEMAE HILL ROLLINS
June 20, 1897–February 2, 1979
Occupation: children's librarian, writer, educator

Charlemae Hill Rollins was born in Holly Springs, Mississippi, in 1897. In 1904, her family migrated to the Oklahoma Territory. There, until she was thirteen years old, Rollins attended Pleasant Hill School, which had been built by her father and where her mother also worked. She was forced to travel to three different states to graduate from high school because there were no high schools for Black children in Oklahoma in the early 1900s. She later obtained a teaching certificate and attended Howard University in Washington, DC.

Rollins started her career as a librarian at the Harding Square Branch of the Chicago Public Library in 1926 and became the first children's librarian at the George Cleveland Hall Branch, the first library on the South Side, when it opened in 1932. By 1939, the library served 95,000 residents in Bronzeville and surrounding neighborhoods.

Rollins remained at Hall for thirty-one years until her retirement. She spoke out against the racist depictions of Black people in children's books, writing her own children's books to counteract those depictions. In addition to continuing her education at Columbia University (1932) and the **University of Chicago** (1934–36), she taught courses at Roosevelt University, including one called "Children's Literature."

MARJORIE STEWART JOYNER'S HOME AND HAIR SALON | 5607 S. Wabash Avenue

MARJORIE STEWART JOYNER

October 24, 1896–December 27, 1994
Occupation: entrepreneur, inventor, educator, civil rights activist, hairstylist

Marjorie Stewart Joyner, who was the granddaughter of enslaved people, was born in Monterey, Virginia, in 1896. She grew up in poverty; in 1904, her family moved to Dayton, Ohio, in search of better opportunities. After her parents divorced, Joyner went to live with her mother in Chicago. She was unable to complete high school because she needed to work to supplement her family's income.

Joyner was a domestic worker and a waitress until she was able to learn beauty culture at the A.B. Mollar Beauty School. She became the first Black graduate of the school in 1916. She met and married Dr. Robert E. Joyner, a well-respected podiatrist, and had two daughters with him.

Joyner started her first hair salon at 5448 S. State Street, initially catering to white women. Her training at the Mollar Beauty School had only taught her how to style white women's hair. After a disastrous attempt to do her mother-in-law's hair, Marjorie paid $17.50 to enroll in Madam C. J. Walker's Chicago beauty school to learn how to style Black hair. Once she learned, her customers included famous performers like Lena Horne, Louis Armstrong, and Billie Holiday.

Impressed with Joyner, Madam Walker recruited her to serve as her national spokesperson and one of her chief advisers. By the time Walker died in 1919, Joyner was the vice president of the company and the national supervisor for the Madam C. J. Walker beauty schools. Joyner oversaw and helped build a network of more than 200 beauty schools across the United

States. She recruited, trained, and managed thousands of "Walker Agents"—women who sold shampoos, hair oils, and straightening combs from their homes and door-to- door. Franchises with the Walker's beauty empire allowed thousands of Black women to launch their own businesses.

In 1928, to make the Marcel Wave (a hairstyle popularized by singer Josephine Baker) easier to create, Joyner invented and filed a patent for a permanent wave machine that became a standard fixture in salons across America. Later, she went on to cofound the United Beauty School Owners and Teachers Association. Joyner spent over fifty years with the Walker company.

A supporter of Black education, Joyner raised thousands of dollars of funding for Black colleges and universities. While her philanthropic, educational, and beauty culture business interests took her around the country and the world, she remained active in Chicago cultural and civic life. She cofounded the Cosmopolitan Community Church and helped to keep it going.

In 1929, Joyner and Robert Sengstacke Abbott, the founder of the *Chicago Defender*, organized the first Bud Billiken Parade, which pays tribute to the mythological protector of Black children. For more than sixty years, she continued to direct the parade as the chair of the *Chicago Defender* Charities. She championed several social justice causes, was good friends

with Eleanor Roosevelt and Mary Mc-Cleod Bethune, and was very active in Democratic politics, providing counsel and major support to Harold Washington. At seventy-seven years old, she decided to go to college and graduated with a bachelor's degree from Bethune-Cookman College.

Institutional affiliations

National Council of Negro Women

Cosmopolitan Community Church

Chicago Defender Charities

Alpha Chi Pi Omega Sorority and Fraternity

United Beauty School Owners and Teacher's Association

Bethune-Cookman College

Additional landmarks and locations

Joyner's first hair salon was located at 5448 S. State Street.

REYNOLDS CLUB (UNIVERSITY OF CHICAGO)
1131 E. 57th Street

GEORGIANA ROSE SIMPSON

1866-1944
Occupation: educator,
professor, scholar

Georgiana Rose Simpson was the first Black woman to receive a PhD from the **University of Chicago**, and one of the first two Black women in the nation to receive a doctorate degree. Simpson was born and raised in Washington, DC, where she started training to become an elementary school teacher. She came to Chicago in 1907 to obtain her bachelor's degree in German language and literature from the University of Chicago.

Simpson experienced extreme racism as she attempted to integrate the university and was forced to move out of the dormitory after the university president, Harry Pratt Judson, demanded her removal. She enrolled in summer courses and took additional classes via correspondence to limit interaction with students who were against integration on campus. In 1911, Simpson completed her bachelor's degree and returned to Washington to teach at Paul Laurence Dunbar High School.

In 1917, Simpson returned to Chicago to pursue her postgraduate degree in German philosophy. She received her PhD from the University of Chicago in 1921, the same year that Sadie Tanner Mossell Alexander received her PhD in economics from the University of Pennsylvania—making them the first two Black women to receive distinguished doctorates in the United States.

Simpson went back to teaching high school and eventually became a professor at Howard University. She remained in touch and exchanged correspondence with other alumni from the University of Chicago, including Carter G. Woodson and **Katherine Dunham**. In 2017, after a student-led effort to honor Simpson, the University of Chicago unveiled a bronze bust of her likeness on the campus at the **Reynolds Club.**

Institutional affiliations

University of Chicago
Howard University
Paul Laurence Dunbar High School

VIOLETTE NEATLEY ANDERSON 🖧
July 16, 1882–December 24, 1937
Occupation: lawyer, court reporter, business owner

ATTORNEY VIOLETTE N. ANDERSON
Highly Honored Member of the Chicago Bar, She Being the Only Colored Woman Practicing at the Bar of Illinois.

Violette Neatley Anderson was born on July 16, 1882, in London, England. When she was a young child, her family immigrated to Chicago, where she grew up and attended public schools. After high school, she studied at the Chicago Athenaeum and the Chicago Seminar of Sciences.

Neatley Anderson worked as a courtroom reporter for fifteen years and managed a court reporting business in Chicago's downtown lawyers' district. She subsequently attended the **University of Chicago** Law School in 1917 and became the first Black woman to graduate from law school in Illinois. She passed the bar exam in 1920. Once licensed, she was one of the first women in Illinois to have her own private law practice.

Neatley Anderson was also the first Black woman to practice law before the US District Court for the Eastern Division of Illinois, and the first Black woman to practice law before the US Supreme Court. She was named the first vice president of the Cook County Bar Association, an organization created in response to discrimination from white lawyers at the Chicago Bar Association.

In 1922, Neatley Anderson successfully defended a woman who was accused of killing her husband—this led to her appointment as the first Black and first female assistant prosecutor in Chicago. She also lobbied actively in favor of the federal Bankhead-Jones Bill to help make low-interest loans available to Black tenant farmers and sharecroppers so they could buy farmland. The bill passed and was signed into law in 1937.

University of Chicago Law School
North Division High School
Northern District of Federated
Women's Clubs

Zeta Phi Beta Sorority
Cook County Bar Association
National Bar Association
Chicago Council of Social Agencies

SPAULDING-SILVER-DUNLAP POLICY WHEEL
7539 S. Indiana Avenue

FLORINE REYNOLDS IRVING STEPHENS 🕯️ ⑤
1913–December 20, 2012
Occupation: entrepreneur, business owner

From the thirties through the fifties, illegal gambling—specifically playing policy or numbers, a game where players placed bets on which numbers would be selected from a large wheel—was widespread in Bronzeville. These activities mostly took place in male-dominated spaces, but some women became important policy entrepreneurs. Discrimination and racial segregation limited the Black community's economic options in Chicago's Black Belt, and the underground economy was one avenue of financial opportunity. The best-known "Queen of Policy" in Chicago was Florine Reynolds Irving Stephens, a wealthy and stylish businesswoman with a fondness for mink coats, who operated multiple policy wheels on the South Side, earning millions of dollars.

Stephens married James D. Irving in March 1937. He was a cab driver at the time, but by 1947, when Stephens filed for divorce, Irving had become the "king" of mid-twentieth-century policy. In the divorce, Stephens received a significant financial settlement. She also received an out-of-court settlement that included one of Irving's policy wheels, the Boulevard-Avenue Wheel, which brought in an estimated $25,000 weekly. In 1955, Irving was sent to federal prison for tax evasion, at which point Stephens was able to expand her business to include several other policy wheels. She married Quincy Stephens, alias Stephenson, a small-time policy operator, in 1950. Quincy teamed up with Florine and her brothers, George and Eugene Reynolds, in the operation of the Boulevard-Avenue Wheel at 3034 S. Indiana Avenue.

On November 30, 1961, the couple, along with Florine's son, James Irving Jr., were arrested in a raid connected to the Spaulding-Silver-Dunlap Policy Wheel, another wheel owned by the couple that was located at 7539 S. Indiana Avenue. The police said that the Spaulding-Silver-Dunlap Wheel netted $14,000 a day, or more than $5 million annually in 1960s money.

While in business, Stephens employed approximately sixty runners who distributed betting slips in small businesses throughout the community and about eight hundred writers to take bets, including many women. The rise of policy wheels created well-paid employment opportunities for Black women, who could earn $20 per week as runners or writers in comparison to the $5–8 per week they might expect to make in kitchens, domestic labor, or manufacturing.

Though gambling itself often had a negative financial influence on individual customers who placed bets, policy wheels like Stephens' businesses created jobs that were less exploitative, discriminatory, and unsafe for Black women than the low-paying domestic work and kitchen labor that were often their only options. Women served as policy runners and writers and placed bets. Women who had disabilities, young, or elderly, could also access money through the underground economy with Stephens' businesses. One elderly player recounted, "My luck got so good, and since I was bothered with rheumatism, I quit the laundry [where I worked]" (Schroeder Schlabach).

While formal economies were frequently unstable and consistently unapproachable for most members of the Black community in Chicago and beyond, Stephens' illegal policy wheels created accessible economic structures by and for Black people. Policy also created possibilities to dream beyond the economic conditions one faced; as such, it made direct appearances in Black literature and other forms of creative expression during the Harlem and Chicago Black Renaissance Art Movements.

Additional landmarks and locations

Boulevard-Avenue Wheel at
3034 S. Indiana Avenue

NATIONAL A. PHILIP RANDOLPH PULLMAN PORTER MUSEUM

10406 S. Maryland Avenue

Located in Chicago's Far South, the Pullman Historic District was the first model-planned industrial town in the United States. The district was initially built in 1880 by the Pullman Palace Car Company and founder George Pullman to manufacture luxury railroad passenger cars and house the company's workers and their families. As the company expanded, so did the district's layout, which ultimately included a firehouse, offices, a school, a bank, and a hotel, in addition to over 1700 homes and a market square for grocery vendors.

African Americans were not permitted to live in the Pullman community in the 1800s and early 1900s, but at its height, the Pullman Company was one of the largest employers of Black workers in the nation. They were predominantly hired as porters and served on almost every major railroad in the country. The porters eventually formed a labor union in the quest for fair wages and improved working conditions.

The Pullman community was declared a National Historic Landmark in 1970, named a Chicago Landmark District in 1972, and designated as a National Monument in 2015.

The Pullman District currently includes the National A. Philip Randolph Pullman Porter Museum, the only Black labor history museum in the nation. The museum was founded in 1995 and named after Asa Philip Randolph, the influential leader of the Brotherhood of Sleeping Car Porters (BSCP).

HELENA WILSON

February 25, 1895–April 16, 1975
Occupation: labor organizer, civil rights
activist, writer

Helena Wilson was a community activist who spent over twenty-five years advancing the labor movement and supporting women's education as president of the International Ladies' Auxiliary of the Brotherhood of Sleeping Car Porters (BSCP). Her leadership was transformative for the national labor movement and the larger cooperative movement.

Born in 1895 in Denver, Colorado, Wilson moved to Chicago in the 1920s. In Chicago, she married Benjamin Wilson, who worked as a sleeping car porter. In the early 1900s, the nation's largest employer of Black workers was Pullman Palace Car Company, which built luxury railway cars and employed personnel to serve affluent white travelers. The maids and sleeping car porters on the Pullman railway cars were almost exclusively Black, many of them formerly enslaved. They were subjected to harsh working conditions, racist treatment, and meager wages that had to be supplemented by tips from the white passengers. These circumstances led to the 1925 formation of the BSCP labor union.

In 1931, Wilson became the president of the Chicago branch of the Colored Women's Economic Council. The council was a network of Brotherhood auxiliary chapters in cities throughout the nation, founded by Pullman porters' wives. The women organized campaigns, raised money, and garnered support from the porters' families and communities. In 1938, Wilson was appointed president of the International Ladies' Auxiliary, a larger coalition of women-led support groups for the Brotherhood. She and the organization spread awareness about labor organizing and fostered support networks to expand the influence of the Brotherhood throughout Black communities to help families in economic distress.

Wilson ensured that the auxiliary provided avenues for adult education about consumer co-ops, credit unions, and financial management. She was also a member of the national Consumer Cooperative Council and helped form the Cooperative Union Eye Care Center and the Cooperative Buying Club in the 1950s. Under her leadership, the auxiliary created the Brotherhood Consumer Cooperative store. It was the first of its kind, founded by Black women connected to the labor movement.

Political involvement was an outgrowth of Wilson's commitment to the auxiliary. She advocated for more employment opportunities and fair housing, as well as antilynching legislation. Her social and political beliefs concerning the ongoing Civil Rights movement, and the role of Black women within the labor movement, are articulated in essays she wrote for the *Black Worker*, the Brotherhood's monthly journal.

Following ten years of fighting for recognition, in 1937, the Brotherhood signed a contract with the Pullman company that provided the Black porters with improved wages and hours. This feat, a historic moment that would forever change the relationship between Black workers and American companies, would not have been possible without the expansive work of Helena Wilson and the International Ladies' Auxiliary.

Institutional affiliations

Colored Women's Economic Council
Brotherhood of Sleeping Car Porters
International Ladies' Auxiliary
Consumers Cooperative Buying Club
Cooperative Union Eye Care Center
Chicago Women's Trade Union League
Consumer Cooperative Council

WEST SIDE

EXCAVATING THE WEST SIDE'S HISTORY

The question we were asked at almost every event we held after publishing the first edition of *Lifting as They Climbed* was, "What about the West Side?" The choice to expand the book to include these West Side women was a complicated one. In comparison to what we were able to excavate on the South Side, there were fewer sources pertaining to Black women who worked in, lived in, and affected the West Side from the late nineteenth to mid-twentieth century. There are two primary reasons for this research challenge. The first is that the patterns of settlement during the Great Migration meant most of the Black population settled on the South Side of Chicago. The second is that there seems to be no comprehensive preservation of West Side histories pertaining to Black women. These obstacles are reflected in the disparity between the quantity of women we feature from the South Side and the much smaller number from the West Side.

A *Chicago Defender* article published in 1913 states that "very few people in speaking of Chicago take into consideration the West Side, which after all, is the largest part of the city and incidentally the oldest part." Over one hundred years later, the description still holds true.

However, there is no history of Chicago without the history of the West Side. To better understand the gaps in the repository of information on Black women's histories, it's important to understand the beginnings of the West Side. The first Black settlements on the West Side date back to 1837, the same year Chicago was incorporated as a city. During this time, of the seventy-seven people comprising the city's African American population, only twenty-two were West Siders. This small enclave of "old settlers" formed along Chicago's Lake Street, known as the Near West Side, and slowly moved further west.

The Negro Family in Chicago by sociologist E. Franklin Frazier, published in 1932, documents the composition and demographics of the earliest African American communities, including the Lake Street settlements. These settlers would remain a very small fraction of the total population throughout the nineteenth century. We document some of the historical traces they left through the lives of physician **Harriett Alleyne Rice** and clubwoman **Willie P. Cherry**.

During the first wave of the Great Migration, the city's total Black population increased by over 65,000, but the West Side Black population only grew by 5,300. Many of the migrants moved to the South Side and were funneled along the city's Black Belt. In a city ill-equipped to accommodate the rapid growth, African Americans faced a housing crisis and scarce employment options exacerbated by racist segregation and social violence. The problems crossed neighborhood lines, but the ways that they were addressed varied from South to West.

While the South Side became a bustling metropolis for a more economically mobile set, the early West Siders were often laborers whose communities were focused on the family unit, with the church as the epicenter. According to Historian Christopher Reed, "Black west siders ended up relying on the family, church, and communal ties to sustain themselves in the face of the disruptive and debilitating influences of urbanism and racism."

The Cherry family, which arrived in Chicago in 1893, is often held up as an influential example of the African American families that lived on the West Side. Although this family's records are helpful in understanding home life and social dynamics in the area during the end of the nineteenth century and throughout the twentieth, they also reflect the patriarchal dynamics of the community and family structures in how they dictate whose stories are captured and whose are lost. For instance, the story of the Cherry family is told through the lens of the father, **Wiley Cherry**. Almost all historical accounts give details about Wiley, but only address his first wife Margaret and second wife Fannie by name, omitting any other descriptors of who they were beyond

their marriage. Willie, his third wife and an active community member, is rarely even mentioned. What remains of the Cherry family history in the archives offers a glimpse of the stories we don't have access to because of gender-biased history-making.

Eventually the Black population on the West Side would experience rapid growth from the 1940s through the 1960s. The Sixties ushered in the Civil Rights Movement, with the West Side becoming a hub for the **Black Panther Party** and political organizing on the Left. In 1968, the assassination of Martin Luther King Jr. would forever change the social and political face of the West Side. The riots, and the political decisions not to rebuild, caused irreparable damage to decades of urban development. Over 250 businesses were destroyed, and hundreds of Chicagoans were injured. What would have been historical landmarks and locations turned into empty lots and abandoned buildings.

Today, the Vivian G. Harsh Research Collection of Afro-American History and Literature at Chicago's Carter G. Woodson Regional Library is a primary source for materials on Black history in Chicago. However, the collection predominantly documents the history of the South Side. The West Side does not have any such expansive archive or public repository of community history. As the distinguished Chicago archivist, Beverly Cook, helped us understand, much of what is left of West Side Black history is in the hearts, minds, attics, and basements of those who remain there. This is not to say that there has been no work to preserve those memories over the past century, but to show how the West Side has lacked the organized collectives and institutional infrastructures of preservation that the South Side has over the decades.

Of all the research compiled for this section, one of the most plentiful repositories of information was the Bethel New Life Records collection, held at the special collections of the Harold Washington Library, the main branch of the Chicago Public Library system. The collection was assembled by the nonprofit organization, Bethel New Life Inc., in 1984 and 1985, as part of a project to center the West Side's Black community in the recovery of the area's history. The collection contains accounts, not only of West Side histories in general, but of the lives of the Black women who lived there. The records posed their own challenges, as some of the oral histories gathered for the project are closed to researchers and won't be released for decades due to legal issues. This struggle reflects the need for a larger, more concerted effort to collect Black women's histories on the West Side. These women and countless others deserve to have their stories amplified and uplifted.

We are building the road as we walk it, and we hope that more histories will be uncovered as we share the bits of history that we do have currently. There are plenty of women whom we would have loved to include but doing so would have required a few more years of research and perhaps an entirely different book. We didn't include other women because their records are unavailable, not yet collected, or altogether nonexistent. We list some of their names below in hopes that someone will read this and reach out, so that more West Side Black women's histories can be captured and shared. They include:

Ma Alice Henry
Sylvia Green Woods
Frances Lee
Iola McGowan
Earlene Lindsey
Fannie B. Woodley

There are countless more. If you know of any, please visit www.LiftingAsTheyClimbed.com and let us know.

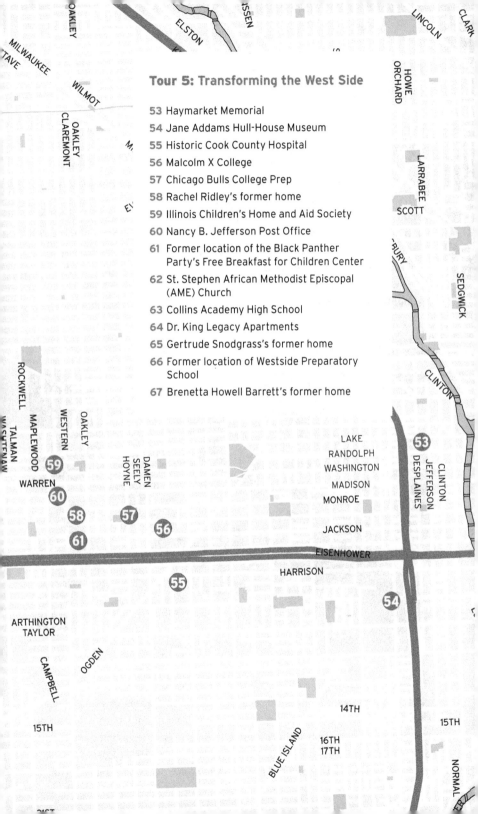

Tour 5: Transforming the West Side

TOUR 5: TRANSFORMING THE WEST SIDE

What is the history of the West Side of Chicago? How do we understand this history in relation to the contributions of Black women? The West Side story we seek to tell through these fifteen women is one that spans over 120 years. This tour takes readers to landmarks across more than six West Side neighborhoods, from the West Loop to the Near West Side, through Garfield Park and Lawndale, to South Austin. Through these sites, we document, among other strains of Chicago history, the education movement started by Marva Collins; the Black Arts Movement and one of its pioneers, **Barbara Jones-Hogu;** and the lifetime of activism embodied by **Brenetta Howell Barrett.** We seek to illuminate the ways Black women upheld their communities, from the solution-oriented brilliance of **Rachel Rebecca Ridley** to the communal dedication of **Gertrude Snodgrass.**

HAYMARKET MEMORIAL | 175 N. Desplaines Street

On May 4, 1886, a group of activists organized a public meeting in Chicago's Haymarket district in response to a deadly labor clash the previous day. Employees had been advocating for better working conditions and an eight-hour workday. When police showed up en masse to the scene of the meeting, conflict arose, and someone threw a deadly bomb. Several civilians and police officers were killed, and numerous others injured. The city responded with a crackdown on the organizers of the meeting, as well as anarchists who had not been present, arresting, trying, and executing several, even though the person who threw the bomb was never identified. The violence and its aftermath garnered international attention.

The Haymarket Memorial, erected in 2004 on Chicago's North Desplaines Street, marks the location where the meeting and bombing occurred. A sculpture created by Mary Brogger represents a broad range of issues connected to the bombing, including workers' rights, the labor movement, and freedom of speech.

LUCY ELDINE GONZALEZ PARSONS (ALSO KNOWN AS LUCY GONZALES)

1853–March 7, 1942
Occupation: labor movement organizer, political and community activist

Lucy Eldine Gonzales Parsons is recognized as one of the most influential women involved in anarchist and labor movements of the late nineteenth and early twentieth centuries. Her racial and ethnic identity has always been a topic of inquiry and mystery to researchers. A recent biography by historian Jacqueline Jones confirms that Parsons was born to an enslaved mother in Virginia in 1851.

Parsons often claimed Indigenous and Mexican ancestry publicly, but never acknowledged her mother's Black identity or the fact that she herself had been born into slavery. She rejected the idea that details of her early years were relevant to her struggles for justice, telling one interviewer, "I am not a candidate for office, and the public have no right to my past. I amount to nothing to the world and people care nothing of me. I am battling for a principle." It is likely that Parsons did not want her identity made public because she feared racism would prevent white working-class people from respecting her political work and heeding her speeches, essays, and calls to unite. Parsons is believed to be the daughter of a white slave master who forced her and her mother to march to Texas during the Civil War. After emancipation, Parsons lived in a common-law marriage with an older man who had also been enslaved. She had a child during this relationship, and was also engaged in a relationship with Albert Parsons, a former white Confederate soldier and Republican Party supporter. Lucy and Albert Parsons married in 1872. Harassment by white supremacists because of their interracial marriage and political work registering Black voters forced them to relocate to Chicago. They arrived there around the time of the 1873 Depression. The economic crisis fueled intense labor unrest that also deeply politicized Parsons, who joined the radical labor movement.

Parsons was a self-taught writer and journalist, who published numerous articles and pamphlets and wrote for *The Alarm*, a newspaper founded by her and her husband. As an organizer, anarchist, and socialist, she led strikes that resulted in the inclusion of Black women in unions. Her speeches commanded large audiences, and she was described as "more dangerous than a thousand rioters" by the Chicago Police Department in 1920.

In 1886, Lucy and Albert Parsons and their two children led Chicago's first May Day march alongside 80,000 workers demanding an eight-hour workday. The same day, over 100,000 workers marched in other cities across the nation. Two days later, on May 3, 1886, when striking workers rallied at the McCormick Reaper Works, the Chicago Police Department arrived and fatally shot protestors. The following day, as labor supporters gathered in Haymarket Square in outrage, a bomb exploded, killing several officers and bystanders.

Though no evidence pointing to who detonated the bomb was ever found, Albert Parsons and other men known as the Haymarket Eight, were charged with murder and conspiracy for the explosion. Lucy Parsons advocated passionately for the release of the Haymarket Eight, touring the country to give speeches about the issue and about workers' rights, but despite her efforts, Albert Parsons was executed in 1887.

Though Parsons was regularly harassed and arrested, she continued to fight against economic, racial, and gender inequalities. She persisted in her struggle until her death in a house fire in 1942. She is buried in the Forest Home Cemetery along with other Haymarket martyrs.

Institutional affiliations

The Alarm, Chicago anarchist newspaper

Industrial Workers of the World

International Ladies' Garment Workers Union

Socialist Labor Party

Haymarket Riots

International Working People's Association

Hull-House

American Federation of Labor

Additional landmarks and locations

Lucy Parsons Park is located at 4712 W. Belmont Avenue.

1908 Mohawk Street is the house where Lucy and Albert's son Albert Jr. was born in 1879.

1901 Larrabee Street is the site of another former home.

1656 Larrabee Street is where the Parsons lived when their daughter Lulu was born in 1881.

1511 Grand Avenue was the Parsons' home in 1884 (they led the Thanksgiving Day "Poor People's Marches" past the mansions on Rush Street and Prairie Avenue when living here).

1374 Grand Avenue was an apartment over a store where they lived in 1885 (they opened a dress shop and tailor shop in the store since they needed to supplement their income).

1120 Grand Avenue was also an apartment over a store where they lived, but after Albert turned himself in to stand trial, Lucy could not afford the rent and moved to 1129 Milwaukee Avenue.

1129 Milwaukee Avenue was occupied by Lucy, Albert Jr., and Lulu in 1887.

3130 N. Troy Street was Lucy's last home.

JANE ADDAMS HULL-HOUSE MUSEUM
800 S. Halsted Street

HARRIET ALLEYNE RICE 🏠📖
January 14, 1866–May 24, 1958
Occupation: physician, writer

Harriet Alleyne Rice battled discrimination to provide medical care to Chicagoans and to Allied forces in World War I. Born in Newport, Rhode Island, in 1866, Rice became the first Black woman to graduate from Wellesley College in Wellesley, Massachusetts, in 1887. She then studied at the University of Michigan Medical School for one year but had to drop out to undergo surgical treatment for an injury she had sustained during her last year at Wellesley. Rice returned to her studies in 1890 at the Woman's Medical College of New York Infirmary for Women and Children and received her MD in 1891.

Rice then relocated to Chicago and became the first Black resident at Hull-House, the famous settlement house that mostly served European immigrants in what is now the city's Near West Side. Between 1893 and 1904, Rice worked on and off in various positions at Hull-House. At times, the white immigrant community that Hull-House served did not welcome her. Though it was an affordable option for housing and provided work opportunities, Rice's relationship with Hull-House founder Jane Addams was sometimes tenuous due to this discrimination.

In 1896, Rice published her first paper, "Tabulation of Records of Cook County Institutions with Notes." The following year, she became the only

doctor at the Chicago Maternity Hospital and Training School for Nursery Maids. Rice faced persistent roadblocks of racist and sexist discrimination as she tried to advance her career. She refused to practice medicine in a racially segregated setting, and because of her convictions she often struggled to make a living as a physician. In 1935, she expressed her despair in response to a survey of Wellesley College alumni, writing, "I'm colored which is worse than any crime in this God blessed Christian country!"

When World War I broke out, Rice applied to join the Red Cross to provide medical services to US troops, but she was denied because of her race. She then went to France, a country more tolerable of African American expatriates, treating soldiers at hospitals during the war and well beyond the war's conclusion. As an expression of gratitude for Rice's tireless work on the front lines, the French government awarded her the bronze medal of Reconnaissance Française in 1919.

American School of Osteopathy	Illinois Board of Charities
Wellesley College	Chicago Maternity Hospital and Training
University of Michigan	School for Nursery Maids
Woman's Medical College of New York	Hull-House
Infirmary for Women and Children	Boston Dispensary

HISTORIC COOK COUNTY HOSPITAL | 1825 W. Harrison Street

The Historic Cook County Hospital building was constructed between 1912 and 1914. The 1.2 million square-foot building was cited as one of the largest hospitals in the world during the early to mid-1900s. According to the National Trust for Historic Preservation Leadership Forum, the hospital "housed the first blood bank in 1937, the nation's first trauma unit in 1966, and one of the first hospitals early on to treat AIDS patients". The building has been featured in blockbuster films and was the setting of the popular television series *ER*.

After the city of Chicago opened a new hospital adjacent to the historic site, the old building closed its doors in 2002. For over a decade, preservation groups advocated to save the building as it stood vacant, slated for demolition. Eventually, the hospital was purchased and underwent a $140 million mixed-use re-development to become the home of, among other things, a Hyatt hotel, a food hall, a museum, and county medical offices.

AGNES LATTIMER

1928–January 9, 2018
Occupation: pediatrician, researcher, activist

Agnes Lattimer was born in Memphis, Tennessee, where she graduated as valedictorian from Booker T. Washington High School. She went on to earn her bachelor's degree in biology from Fisk University in Nashville. After college, Lattimer decided to continue her medical education in Chicago, where she had family; she initially worked as a housekeeper to save money for her studies.

Lattimer began at Chicago Medical School in 1950; she was the only Black woman there and one of only two women. After graduating, she did her internship and residency with **Cook County Hospital** in 1954 and served as chief resident in pediatrics at Chicago's Michael Reese Hospital until 1956. She began her private pediatrics practice shortly thereafter.

Lattimer researched lead poisoning treatment and was respected for her knowledge of the effects of lead poisoning on child development. In addition to providing care directly, she advocated for quality health care for low-income communities. Lattimer also held several prominent leadership positions. She was the associate medical director of ambulatory care at Cook County Hospital. Later, she was director of Cook County Fantus Health Center, which comprised several outpatient clinics.

In 1986, Lattimer was appointed Cook County Hospital's medical director, a position she held until 1995. It is the accomplishment for which she is best known, since she was the first Black woman to head a major hospital in the US.

Institutional affiliations

Fisk University
Cook County Hospital
Chicago Committee Against Lead Poisoning
Michael Reese Hospital
Cook County Fantus Health Center
Chicago Medical School
American Academy of Pediatrics
University of Chicago

MALCOLM X COLLEGE | 1900 W. Jackson Boulevard

Malcolm X College is on Chicago's Near West Side. Originally named Crane Junior College from 1911 to 1934, it was the first junior college in Chicago and grew to be the largest in the nation. The Great Depression led to a brief closure, but the school reopened as Herzl Junior College a year later. In 1968, at the height of the Civil Rights era, community members advocated for the school to be renamed after Malcolm X. It has since changed locations and is currently designated as the center of excellence in health care education for City Colleges of Chicago.

BARBARA JONES-HOGU
April 17, 1938–November 14, 2017
Occupation: painter, printmaker, educator

Born in Chicago on April 17, 1938, Barbara Jones-Hogu was a pioneering visual artist in the Black Arts Movement. Also an educator, she was a founding member of AfriCOBRA (the African Commune of Bad Relevant Artists).

A lifetime resident of Chicago with a deep commitment to education, Jones-Hogu obtained bachelor's degrees from Howard University and the School of the Art Institute of Chicago. She then earned a Master of Fine Arts from the Institute of Design in Chicago, followed by a master's degree in printing from the Illinois Institute of Technology. Beyond personal pursuits, Jones-Hogue was a lifelong educator, teaching in Chicago Public Schools as well as becoming an associate professor at Malcolm X College, where she taught for nearly three decades.

As an artist, Jones-Hogu was a member of the Organization of Black American Culture (OBAC). In 1967, she contributed to the creation of the Wall of Respect (1967-1971) in Chicago, one of the first large-scale outdoor murals in the United States. The celebrated mural depicted prominent African American figures and scenes of Black historical uplift, which sparked a global monument movement.

A year later, Jones-Hogu joined four other artists to create Afri-COBRA, a nationally renowned art collective. AfriCOBRA's artwork centered on themes of Black power, liberation, and cultural pride, and was popularized through the Civil Rights Movement, becoming a groundbreaking collective of the Black Arts Movement. Jones-Hogu and the AfriCOBRA artists were featured in exhibitions around the world.

As an influential member of the group, Jones-Hogu wrote parts of its 1969 manifesto "Ten in Search of a Nation." Her signature aesthetic included bold lettering in combination with the collective's strong messaging related to Black resistance and unified struggle. She was instrumental in expanding the visual accessibility of the collective's artwork through her knowledge and use of screen printing. Her skills amplified AfriCOBRA's reach and paved the way for the mass distribution of each artist's work.

In her early seventies, Jones-Hogu returned to graduate school to study independent filmmaking at Governors State University. Her artwork is held in multiple public museum collections around the nation, including the Art Institute of Chicago, the National Civil Rights Museum, the National Museum of African American Culture and History, and the Brooklyn Museum.

Institutional affiliations

AfriCOBRA
Art Institute of Chicago
Illinois Institute of Technology
Organization of Black American Culture
South Side Community Arts Center

CHICAGO BULLS COLLEGE PREP (FORMERLY CREGIER VOCATIONAL HIGH SCHOOL) | 2040 W. Adams Street

Cregier High School opened in 1957 on the city's West Side to alleviate overcrowding at nearby schools. The original building was located at 1820 W. Grenshaw Street, until the school was moved to 2040 W. Adams Street in 1980. The school closed in 1995 and is the current site of Chicago Bulls College Prep.

ANNABEL CAREY PRESCOTT

February 13, 1894-July 29, 1982
Occupation: educator, civil rights activist, researcher

Dr. Annabel Carey Prescott dedicated her life to education and worked for the Chicago Public Schools for forty-two years. She began as a teacher at Doolittle Elementary School and retired as the director of the Department of Human Relations for Chicago Public Schools.

Carey Prescott was born in 1894, into what would become one of the most well-known families in Chicago's Black "old settler" community. Her father was a pastor at the largest African Methodist Episcopal (AME) church in Chicago, Quinn Chapel. She attended two Chicago public schools that she would later return to as an educator.

During her career, Carey Prescott worked in several schools. In 1935, she was the chair of the French department at **Wendell Phillips Academy High School** on the South Side until she was promoted to become the second African American dean of girls in the school's history. Carey Prescott eventually left Phillips to take a position as assistant principal at **DuSable High School**. In 1941, she took a brief leave of absence to work on her master's degree at DePaul University. Carey Prescott continued her studies, pursuing a PhD in intergroup relations from Columbia University. Her work as assistant principal of **Cregier High School** served as the foundation for her doctoral dissertation.

During the early 1950s, the demographics on the West Side were rapidly changing. As Black, Latino, and immigrant children were integrating previously segregated schools in impoverished neighborhoods, racial tension increased. Through a pilot program at three public schools, Carey Prescott used community civics classes and human relations concepts to combat intolerance and racial hostility. The program's success garnered her national attention and local support to continue implementing it. In 1956, she developed cultural competency training courses for West Side teachers.

Carey Prescott worked with Chicago community organizations and fought for civil rights. She was appointed to the education committee of the Mayor's Commission on Human Relations and became a member of the executive committee of the Women's Council on Fair Education. In 1965, she was appointed to the Illinois State Board of Junior Colleges. She taught educators at Northwestern University, the **University of Chicago**, Marquette University, and the University of Wisconsin. Over the course of her career, she won numerous awards for her contributions to human relations and education.

Institutional affiliations

South Side Community Arts Center
Wendell Phillips Academy High School
DuSable High School
Medill High School
McKinley High School (Cregier branch)
Department of Human Relations for Chicago Public Schools
Illinois Junior College Board
Fulbright Foreign Teacher Exchange Program
Chicago Urban League
Anti-Defamation League

RACHEL RIDLEY'S FORMER
HOME | 2345 W. Monroe Street

RACHEL REBECCA RIDLEY
April 10, 1911–May 3, 1986
Occupation: community leader, organizer, institution builder

Rachel Rebecca Ridley, a renowned community organizer and administrator, was the driving force behind the establishment of multiple community-centered organizations. She developed programs to support women and girls and organized the West Side to create block clubs to address the environmental and social problems faced by migrants to the neighborhood.

Ridley was born in Hannibal, Missouri. In 1918, her family moved to Chicago's West Side, where she would live for the rest of her life. In 1927, while attending McKinley High School, she began working in the community through her involvement with St. Stephen AME Church. One of Ridley's first jobs was with the Federal Adult Education Project, where she taught literacy skills to adults. In 1947, she helped to develop a program that would eventually become the MidWest Community Council, a community safety organization. She was elected president of the Mid-West Community Council in 1954 and helped to establish its foundations.

She also worked for the Chicago

Urban League, organizing youth groups on the West Side, and was eventually promoted to director of the Urban League's West Side Center. Ridley's efforts were focused on the organization's Women's Division, and, according to environmental epidemiologist Sylvia Hood Washington, she became "the creative and organizing force" in the development of West Side neighborhood block clubs. The block clubs, which began as a project of the Urban League, were micro-formations developed to provide social support and alleviate hardships that plagued African Americans migrating into overcrowded, under-resourced communities.

Ridley became the director of the West Side office of the *Chicago Defender* for two years, after which she took a position with the Chicago Commission on Human Relations within the Department of Community Service. Ridley developed community councils and served as a consultant to community groups in Lawndale, Euclid Park, the Near North Side, and several other neighborhoods throughout Chicago.

In the 1960s, Ridley held several leadership positions in multiple organizations, including the Chicago Commission on Youth Welfare, the Chicago Committee on Urban Opportunity, and Englewood Urban Progress Center. In 1968, she rejoined the Commission on Human Relations, where she created Project Girls. The program reached nearly 8,000 teenaged girls, providing access to employment opportunities and workshops on health, wellness, financial literacy, and human relations.

Ridley's work and leadership in the community earned her many awards and recognitions throughout her lifetime. Chicago Mayor Jane Bryne described Ridley as "a pioneer in women's rights and human rights who always worked at getting people to work together."

Institutional affiliations

Chicago Urban League
Chicago Commission on Human Relations
Operation PUSH
Federal Poverty Program
Chicago Commission on Youth Welfare
Chicago Defender
University of Chicago
Roosevelt University
Crane Junior College
Lewis Institute
Chicago City College
Englewood Urban Process Center
Chicago Committee on Urban Opportunity
Manpower
National Association of Club Women
Alpha Gamma Pi

Additional landmarks and locations

Chicago Defender West Side offices, 2400 W. Madison Street

St. Stephen African Methodist Episcopal Church, 3042 W. Washington Boulevard

ILLINOIS CHILDREN'S HOME AND AID SOCIETY
100 N. Western Avenue

A leading child and family services agency in Illinois, with locations around Chicago and throughout Illinois, the Illinois Children's Home and Aid Society, provides support for homeless and dependent children and their families, including adoption, foster care, boarding, counseling, and other social services.

EDITH SPURLOCK SAMPSON 💼 ⛓
October 13, 1901–October 8, 1979
Occupation: judge, social worker, lawyer,
international civil rights activist

Edith Spurlock Sampson was a trailblazing lawyer, judge, and civil rights activist. She was one of the first African American women admitted to practice before the US Supreme Court, the first Black US delegate appointed to the United Nations, and the first Black woman elected as a judge in Illinois.

Sampson was born in Pittsburgh, Pennsylvania, in 1901. After high school, she joined the Associated Charities of Pittsburgh. The organization provided her with support to attend the New York School of Social

Work. Although one of her professors encouraged her to attend law school, Sampson didn't immediately take his advice.

After graduating with her degree in social work, she married Rufus Sampson. Together they moved to Chicago, where Edith worked at the School of Social Service Administration at the **University of Chicago**. She worked with the **Illinois Children's Home and Aid Society** and the YMCA to provide support for children experiencing neglect and abuse. She ultimately divorced Rufus Sampson and later went on to marry Joseph Clayton, a Chicago attorney.

In 1925, Sampson was awarded a law degree from John Marshall Law School. After failing her first bar exam, she enrolled in Loyola University Law School and graduated with a Master of Law. By 1927, Sampson had opened a law firm on the South Side of Chicago. There, she would provide legal aid to vulnerable populations, especially impoverished Black women. She also organized a small group of Black women lawyers to offer free legal services to women with financial challenges.

In 1934, Sampson was among the first African American women admitted to practice law before the US Supreme Court. In 1947, she was the first Black woman appointed assistant state's attorney for Cook County, turning her law office over to two young Black women lawyers as a legal clinic for poor Chicagoans.

In 1950, Sampson became the first Black woman to be appointed

as a US representative to the United Nations. She served on the UN General Assembly's Social, Humanitarian, and Cultural Affairs Committee, where she worked on land reform and the repatriation of prisoners of war, among other issues. Sampson was an international leader with the National Council of Negro Women and served as a spokesperson for the US State Department throughout the 1950s.

During her travels around the world, Sampson took on an increasingly internationalist perspective and began to advocate for the unification of women of color globally. She also used her international platforms to push for the end of racial discrimination in the United States and abroad. However, she received criticism from some other Black activists for her vocal support of American democracy and her anticommunist sentiments.

In 1962, Sampson became the first Black woman elected as a judge in Illinois, taking a seat on the Chicago Municipal Court. In 1966, she became the first Black woman to sit on the Circuit Court of Cook County. She provided counsel to numerous presidents, other federal officials, and first ladies on issues of social justice and civil rights. At the community level, she mentored Black women and girls and encouraged them to pursue positions of power.

Additional landmarks and locations

Edith Spurlock Sampson Apartments, 2640 N. Sheffield Avenue

NANCY B. JEFFERSON POST OFFICE | 116 S. Western Avenue

NANCY B. JEFFERSON

1923–October 18, 1992
Occupation: community organizer, social services activist

Nancy B. Jefferson was known as one of the most influential grassroots organizers in the United States. In 1963, she started her activism in Chicago as a volunteer for the MidWest Community Council, the oldest community-based social action group on the West Side. She went on to become deeply involved in the group for twenty-five years, serving as its Chief Executive Officer, Executive Director, and President.

Jefferson joined with other West Side organizers to fight corruption and discrimination by powerful political and corporate actors. In the fall of 1988, she was one of a group of activists threatening to declare "open war" on City Hall after Mayor Eugene Sawyer awarded a city contract to the nephew of a Chicago alderman. The following year, Jefferson fought against the discriminatory hiring practices of Chicago-based Quaker Oats Company in management and board appointments.

Jefferson also worked to build an organized West Side network of one hundred block clubs to promote cultural and spiritual exchange, as well as the physical development of the community. She fostered community interventions through social programs like the Chicago Parent Union and Crime and Parent Intervention. Jefferson helped form the Chicago West Side Project, a group of thirty of downtown Chicago's most powerful stakeholders. The group met quarterly to discuss sociopolitical and economic issues facing the city in general and the West Side in particular.

Her sustained efforts to rebuild the area after the depredations from race riots, hate crimes, and arson in the 1960s ensured that Jefferson would be remembered as the "Mother of the West Side." Her work uplifted her community and created accessible interventions for the West Side— or, as she called it, the "best side"—of Chicago.

Institutional affiliations

MidWest Community Council
Chicago Parent Union
Crime and Parent Intervention
Chicago West Side Project

Additional landmarks and locations

Nancy B. Jefferson Boulevard
Nancy B. Jefferson Alternative School
1100 S. Hamilton Avenue

FORMER LOCATION OF THE BLACK PANTHER PARTY'S FREE BREAKFAST FOR CHILDREN CENTER
Jackson Boulevard Christian Church, 2413 W. Jackson Boulevard

The Black Panther Party (BPP) is one of the most renowned African American leftist revolutionary organizations in history. The organization was founded in 1966 in Oakland, California by Huey P. Newton and Bobby Seale, and was originally named the Black Panther Party for Self-Defense. The Panthers implemented nationwide social services and community programs, including free breakfast for children, medical clinics, clothing distribution, and community classes on politics and economics. They advocated for self-defense and organized armed patrols to protect Black community members from police violence. At its height, the party had thousands of members in major cities throughout the United States and worldwide.

In 1968, the Illinois Chapter of the Black Panther Party was formed on the West Side of Chicago. In July 1969, the group opened the Breakfast for Children Center at 2413 W. Jackson Boulevard, which served over two hundred children on its opening day. The chapter's free breakfast program continued to serve hundreds of children throughout the city daily.

During the early 1970s, the FBI targeted the BPP by launching COINTELPRO, a series of illegal operations that led to the murders and arrests of the party's members. These external attacks contributed to the declining political force of the organization.

JOAN FOSTER MCCARTY

b. 1949–

Occupation: organizer, educator, theater professional

Joan Foster McCarty is a former **Black Panther Party** member, an active community organizer, educator, and theater professional. She was born in Chicago's Altgeld Gardens in 1949. McCarty experienced racism at a young age as the only Black student in her classes after her family was one of the first to integrate Bennett Elementary School. In 1966, McCarty enrolled at the University of Illinois Chicago as one of the only Black students in the theater program there. She led the Black Student Organization, connecting with Black students who faced racism in classrooms and on campus at a time when the university offered them no resources or support.

In 1969, McCarty's sister became involved in work against police brutality and community organizing after her partner was killed by members of the Chicago Police Department. This led to McCarty's interest in the Black Panther Party. That same year, she hosted a Huey Newton birthday celebration on the university campus that was attended by BPP leaders Fred Hampton and Bobby Seale. Those interested in joining the BPP had to demonstrate a rigorous level of intellectual commitment. McCarty and all prospective members were required to go six weeks without missing a political education class, as well as the requirements of studying Marxism and Leninism and learning the party's Ten-Point Platform. After being accepted as a member, she participated in weekly meetings at the organization's headquarters on the West Side. McCarty organized party activities and rose early each morning to work in the Free Breakfast Program.

By the seventies, women made up the largest demographic in the organization. Pivotal members of the Illinois chapter who worked in Chicago at the same time as McCarty included Wanda Ross, Yvonne King, Lynn French, Berlina Brewer, Brenda Harris, Akua Njeri, and Donna Calvin. These women managed logistics for events and organized free food giveaways, chapter meetings, and rallies, while also developing connections with other local community assemblies.

During this time, McCarty taught political education classes and considered herself a foot soldier for the BPP, lending a hand where needed in various areas. One of her main responsibilities was managing the party's free busing-to-prisons program in Illinois. The program helped to sustain connections between prisoners and their families by providing free transportation to Illinois penal institutions including Joliet, Stateville, Pontiac, Menard, and Dwight prisons. In 1972, McCarty was one of the key members of the party's De Mau Mau Defense Committee. She ended her work with the BPP in 1975 but continued working with Black and oppressed communities.

As an educator, McCarty served as a teaching artist at the Dwight women's prison and worked at Cabrini-Green Alternative High School.

She also founded the Lumumba Jackson School with strategist and organizer Marion Stamps. For over thirty-five years, McCarty has been a member of the Actors' Equity Association and a stage manager at numerous theaters including Victory Gardens Theater and the Black Ensemble Theater in Chicago, the Milwaukee Repertory Theater, and Atlanta's Theatrical Outfit.

In 1994, McCarty moved to Atlanta, Georgia, where she is currently a professor in the theater and performance department at Spelman College and teaches a class on the history of women in the Black Panther Party.

Institutional affiliations

Lumumba Jackson School
Carbrini-Green Alternative High School
Spelman College
Actors' Equity Association
Harlan High School
Bennett Elementary School
University of Illinois Chicago
Victory Gardens Theater
Black Ensemble Theater
Milwaukee Repertory Theater
Theatrical Outfit

JOAN GRAY 🏢 ✏ 🔗

b. July 29, 1949–
Occupation: activist, dancer, arts administrator

Black Panther activist, dancer, and arts administrator Joan Gray was born in Chicago in 1949, one of eight children. She attended Chicago public schools through her formative years and studied at North Central College in Naperville, Illinois. Gray transferred to a music program at Roosevelt University, where she was recruited into the **Black Panther Party** by Illinois chapter leader Fred Hampton. As a member of the party, she would regularly attend public events with Hampton and recruit women in attendance who were interested in joining.

Entrenched in the BPP's work, Gray helped to organize community programs and was a part of the security staff. In addition, she was instrumental in the Free Breakfast for Children program on the South Side, while her friend and fellow party member, Rhonda Ross, managed it on the West Side. Gray collected donation items from restaurants and stores and prepared them for distribution. To spread awareness and increase access, she also traveled to Chicago housing projects and other communities to talk to residents about the breakfast program.

Gray also traveled to Los Angeles, California, to work in conjunction with the West Coast chapter members. At the local level, she spent time helping to manage the Panther's free health clinic on Chicago's West Side,

where volunteer doctors from neighborhoods around the city would provide treatment for West Side community members without access to health care.

Gray incorporated her passion for music with her community work, teaching piano lessons to youth on the West Side during her time in the BPP. As Gray's activism subsided, her main focus became music performance and dance education. From 1984 to 1991, she was a member of Chicago's Muntu Dance Theater, becoming the troupe president in 1987.

For over ten years, Gray sat on the board of the International Association of Blacks in Dance. She also was a part of the African American Arts Alliance and the Chicago Dance Coalition. To this day, she lives in Chicago.

Institutional affiliations

Black Panther Party
Hyde Park High School
Roosevelt University
International Association of Blacks in Dance
African American Arts Alliance
Chicago Dance Coalition
Muntu Dance Theater

ST. STEPHEN AFRICAN METHODIST EPISCOPAL (AME) CHURCH | 3042 W. Washington Boulevard

St. Stephen African Methodist Episcopal Church was organized in 1872 and is one of the oldest Black churches on the West Side. During the nineteenth and early twentieth centuries, religious institutions on the West Side served as an epicenter for collective moral, social, and civic cultivation.

WILLIE P. CHERRY 🏛 🎓
Date of Birth unknown–April 24, 1959
Occupation: clubwoman, civic worker,
Sunday school teacher

The Cherry family is historically one of the most documented Black families on the West Side of Chicago. Wiley Cherry came from North Carolina to Chicago with his first wife, Margaret, and their children in 1893. They represented what historian Christopher Reed describes as "the quintessential west side family." Wiley Cherry started out as a grocer and went on to open a coal and ice hauling, moving,

and plastering business at 2547 W. Lake Street.

The full details of Willie P. Cherry's life are missing from the record. She was the third wife of Wiley Cherry, patriarch of the West Side Cherry family. Many historical accounts discuss Wiley Cherry, his family, and his two previous wives, but few mention Willie. The main documentation of her life is found in materials donated to the Chicago Public Library's Bethel New Life Collection by her step-granddaughter, Lorraine Heflin.

It is known that Cherry was originally from Athens, Alabama. She graduated from Athens's Trinity College and became a teacher. She and her first husband, Joseph C. Baker, started a family and moved to Chicago in 1900. One of the first organizations that Cherry became involved in was St. Stephen AME Church, one of the oldest churches on the West Side. There, she taught Sunday school, worked as a stewardess, and became

a member of the church's Silent Workers Club.

She married Wiley Cherry in 1915 and raised his children from a previous marriage. Outside her work with the St. Stephen AME church, Cherry was a longtime organizer on the West Side. She became a member of the West Side Women's Club, a politically influential organizing force that supported the needs of incoming migrants, addressed issues of neighborhood improvement and provided resources for community members. She also held various roles in the Forester Fraternities, and Household of Ruth.

Institutional affiliations

West Side Women's Club
St. Stephen AME Church
Household of Ruth
Forester Fraternities

COLLINS ACADEMY HIGH SCHOOL | 1313 S. Sacramento Drive

CARDISS COLLINS

September 24, 1931–February 3, 2013
Occupation: congresswoman, political organizer

Cardiss Collins was a political leader and the first Black woman to be elected to Congress from Illinois and the Midwest. She served twenty-four years in the US House of Representatives, becoming one of the longest-serving women in the history of Congress. Collins was a fierce advocate for women's rights, health care expansion, and equal opportunities for Black and other minority workers and business owners.

Collins was born in 1931 in St. Louis, Missouri. She moved with her parents to Detroit, Michigan, at a young age. After graduating from high school, she moved to Chicago to study business at Northwestern University. She began her professional career working for the State of Illinois Department of Labor and later became a revenue auditor for the state.

Collins's political activism started with her role as a committee member for Chicago's Democratic ward organization. In 1958, she married George Washington Collins; she supported his involvement in politics by participating in his campaigns for alderman, committee member, and ultimately US representative. When her husband died in a tragic plane crash in 1972, Collins was encouraged to run for his vacant congressional seat. She did and won by a large margin to become the fourth Black woman elected to the US Congress.

Over the course of her career, Collins fought tirelessly for racial justice. She spearheaded national affirmative action programs and other policies to create fair hiring practices for Black workers and equal opportunities for minority-owned businesses. For decades, she was a leading figure in the struggle for women's rights, seeking gender and racial equality in broadcast licensing and overseeing investigations that pushed colleges and universities to improve opportunities for female athletes.

Collins authored numerous laws for the safety and health of women and children. She shifted the national consciousness on breast cancer by writing the law that increased Medicare coverage to include mammography testing for women with disabilities and the elderly. She also authored the legislation designating the month of October as National Breast Cancer Awareness Month, and co-founded African American Women for Reproductive Freedom, an organization formed to expand support for reproductive rights.

Collins held several prestigious committee appointments, becoming the first woman and African American person elected as a Democratic whip-at-large and the second woman to chair the Congressional Black Caucus (CBC). During her twenty-three years in Congress, she would shift the course of history for disadvantaged communities throughout the nation. She retired in 1996 and died in 2013 from complications of pneumonia.

Institutional affiliations

NAACP

African American Women for Reproductive Freedom

Chicago Urban League

National Coalition of 100 Black Women

Black Women's Agenda

National Council of Negro Women

24th Ward Democratic Organization

Additional landmarks and locations

Cardiss Collins Post Office, 433 W. Harrison Street

DR. KING LEGACY APARTMENTS | 1550 S. Hamlin Avenue

Dr. King Legacy Apartments are located on the site of Dr. Martin Luther King Jr.'s 1966 residence in the Lawndale neighborhood of Chicago. Organizer and educator **Bobbie L. Steele**, a Lawndale resident for over fifty-six years, writes about taking her children to the site during King's famous 1966 visit in her autobiography, *Woman of Steele: A Personal and Political Journey*. She lived with her husband and children in an apartment just three blocks from the landmark. Unfortunately, her family's home burned down in a 1985 fire.

BOBBIE L. STEELE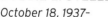

October 18, 1937–
Occupation: commissioner, educator, political organizer

Bobbie L. Steele is a political organizer, an educator, and the longest-serving African American woman in the history of the Cook County government.

Steele was born in Cleveland, Mississippi, in 1937. She left Mississippi after high school to attend college in Alabama, then moved to Chicago's West Side in 1956. It was there that she met and married Robert Steele. The two were married for fifty-two years and had seven children.

Steele overcame several personal and financial challenges early in her career. After the birth of her first two children, she enrolled in Chicago Teachers College. Committed to continuing her education, she took ten years to complete her studies as she gave birth to five more children while juggling full-time work and night classes. She received her bachelor's degree in elementary education in 1966, and shortly afterward started her first teaching position in Chicago Public Schools.

Steele's career in education lasted for twenty-six years, during which she was also active in community and political organizing. The mayoral election of Harold Washington was a turning point for her; he selected her as one of the first women to serve on the Commission on Women's Affairs. During her time collaborating with the mayor, she served on the Employment Committee and worked to increase the representation of women in Chicago's workforce.

In 1986, Steele was elected to the Cook County Board of Commissioners. In her position, she fought to advance employment opportunities for minorities and women, quality health care, and fair taxation. Steele became the first African American woman to serve as chair of the finance committee of the Forest Preserve District. In 2006, she made history once more by becoming the first female president of the Cook County Board of Commissioners.

Institutional affiliations

National Organization of Black County Officials

National Association of Counties Deferred Compensation Committee

Illinois Counties Association

Mt. Hebron Church

Alpha Kappa Alpha

The Links, Inc.

National Council of Negro Women

Illinois Women's Institute for Leadership

Chicago Women's Center

AIDS Foundation of Chicago

Cook County Democratic Women's Organization

Chicago Teachers Union

GERTRUDE SNODGRASS'S FORMER HOME
3906 W. Congress Parkway

GERTRUDE SNODGRASS

November 15, 1913–May 1980
Occupation: institution builder,
humanitarian

Gertrude Snodgrass was born in Alabama in 1913. She came to Chicago during the Great Migration with her husband, Morgan Snodgrass, and their daughter Margaret, but many of the specific details of her origins and life remain a mystery.

What does appear in historical records shows Snodgrass as a caring public servant who was always available to help people in need, from setting up a free clothing shop in a church basement, to providing home-cooked meals for a community shelter, to setting up a food pantry in her Garfield Park home. She left a legacy as one of the co-founders and board members of the Greater Chicago Food

Depository. At a time when there was very little financial support for the depository and only three people on staff, Snodgrass helped keep the organization afloat, working with volunteers and using her home as a space for food processing and canning.

Despite co-founding what remains one of the largest distributors of food to low-income communities in the nation, and despite her personal contributions to feeding thousands of people and providing decades of support for those in need throughout Chicago, Snodgrass is buried in an unmarked grave at Queen of Heaven Cemetery in Hillside, Illinois.

Institutional affiliations

Convent Community Organization Food Pantry

Presentation of the Blessed Virgin Mary Church

Franciscan Outreach

Additional landmarks and locations

Chicago Greater Food Depository, 4100 W. Ann Lurie Place

FORMER LOCATION OF WESTSIDE PREPARATORY SCHOOL | 4146 Chicago Avenue

MARVA COLLINS
August 31, 1936–June 24, 2015
Occupation: educator, institution builder, organizer

Marva Collins was a renowned educator and author who founded **Westside Preparatory School**. Her successful teaching strategies, as described in her book *Marva Collins' Way*, garnered national attention, and were implemented in educational trainings throughout the United States.

Collins was born on August 31, 1936, in Monroeville, Alabama, to a family that highly valued education.

Her father, businessman Alex Nettles, helped to build confidence and a sense of responsibility that she would carry throughout her life. Collins attended Clark College in Atlanta and received a bachelor's degree in secretarial sciences. Following graduation, she returned to Alabama and taught typing, bookkeeping, and business law for two years at Monroe County Training School.

In 1959, Collins moved to Chicago to take a position as a medical secretary at Mount Sinai Hospital. Soon after, she met and married Clarence Collins, a draftsman. In 1961, propelled by her passion for education, Collins began working in the Chicago Public School system. She spent the next fourteen years as a public school teacher. Her disillusionment with the quality of education and teacher engagement in public and private schools motivated her to create her own institution.

In 1975, Collins started teaching a small group of students in the basement of Daniel Hale Williams University. Soon after, she used her pension to renovate the second floor of her home to start the Westside Preparatory School. The school sought to serve students from marginalized communities. Collins expanded into a larger building that would eventually accommodate over two hundred students.

Collins focused on youth flagged as having learning disabilities and behavioral challenges, using a combination of nurturing support and conscientious discipline to strengthen student-learning outcomes. Her methods proved highly successful, and the school attracted the attention of several national publications and television programs. Her students were known to graduate, attend top universities, and thrive in their careers.

The recipient of countless awards, Collins had her life's work and story featured in numerous national publications, ultimately being named a Legendary Woman of the World by the city of Birmingham. Two consecutive US presidents offered her the position of Secretary of Education; she declined, remaining focused on developing the preparatory school and sharing her methodology with educators around the world. In 1981, Hallmark created a film about Collins's life starring Cicely Tyson.

Collins believed that "all children are born achievers and all they need is someone to help them become all that they have the potential to become".

Institutional affiliations

Chicago Public Schools
Monroe County Training School
Mount Sinai Hospital

More to read

Marva Collins' Way by Marva Collins and Civia Tamarkin (TarcherPerigee, 1990)

Ordinary Children, Extraordinary Teachers by Marva Collins (Hampton Roads Publishing, 1992)

BRENETTA HOWELL BARRETT'S FORMER HOME
4923 W. Washington Boulevard

BRENETTA HOWELL BARRETT

June 28, 1932-

Occupation: community organizer, journalist, political activist, founder

Brenetta Howell Barrett has spent over sixty years as a community organizer on the West Side. She is a longtime journalist and founder of multiple organizations created to address equal rights and economic justice for Chicago communities.

Barrett was born in 1932 as Brenetta Pearl Brooks. After skipping a grade at Forestville Elementary, she enrolled in **DuSable High School**. After graduating, she took classes at Century College of Medical Technology and continued her studies at St. Mary's Hospital School of Nursing in Kankakee, Illinois. Barrett married Lessie L. Howell in 1951. The couple had four children and raised them in the North Lawndale neighborhood on Chicago's West Side.

During the 1950s, Barrett was hired by the *Lawndale Booster*. She worked

as a columnist and editor, and eventually became associate editor while also organizing community initiatives for the publication. Barrett would continue her journalism career with other local newspapers, including the *Chicago Enterprise*, *West Town Journal*, *The Star*, *West Side Gazette*, and *Austin Voice*. She eventually managed the *Chicago Defender*'s West Side office and wrote a weekly news column.

During the Civil Rights Movement, Barrett helped found the Chicago Freedom Movement, a coalition of the Southern Christian Leadership Conference (SCLC) and the Coordinating Council of Community Organizations (CCCO). To protest school overcrowding and segregation, Barrett formed the Westside Parents Council for Integrated Schools. In 1964, she became regional director for the NAACP, and fought to launch its West Side branch.

Barrett was on the front lines of the gender equality and women's empowerment movement of the sixties and seventies. She collaborated with Illinois Citizens for the Medical Control of Abortion and the Abortion Rights Association of Illinois to advocate for reproductive rights and spread awareness about Roe v. Wade. She was a co-founder of the League of Black Women and founded Black Sisters United with **Nancy B. Jefferson**, **Edith Spurlock Sampson**, and others.

Entrenched in political activism, Barrett worked on the campaigns of prominent leaders. She became the director of the Governor's Office of Human Resources and was appointed to the cabinet of Illinois Governor Daniel Walker. She was also the Illinois chair of the Shirley Chisholm for President Committee and was the campaign vice president for the mayoral campaign of Harold Washington. After he was elected mayor, Washington appointed Barrett commissioner of the City of Chicago Department of Consumer Services. In 1975, she was the first executive director of the Chicago Black United Fund. In this position, she helped provide grant opportunities to Black community organizations.

As the HIV/AIDS epidemic raged on in the 1990s, Barrett organized on various fronts to establish health care and anti-violence initiatives for the health of West Side communities affected by the disease. She was hired as the executive director of the Illinois branch of the National Abortion and Reproductive Rights Action League. Barrett later went on to found Pathfinders Prevention Education, which offered education, training, and counseling to prevent HIV and other sexually transmitted diseases in multiple West Side neighborhoods.

Barrett continues to organize for West Side communities to this day.

Institutional affiliations

Marcy Center Settlement House

Lawndale Booster

Chicago Urban League

West Side Parents Council for Integrated Schools

Chicago Freedom Movement

Congress of Racial Equality

NAACP

Chicago Economic Development Corporation

West Side Builders Association

Chicago Independent Transportation Survey

League of Black Women

Affairs Unlimited

Austin Voice

Chicago Enterprise

West Side Gazette

Chicago Defender

Black United Fund

Westside Association for Community Action

Congressional Black Caucus

National Association of Black Consumer Organizations

SPECIALIZED TOURS

WRITERS

MUSIC

ACTIVISTS

South Side

BIBLIOGRAPHY

Addams, Jane. 2017. *The Selected Papers of Jane Addams Vol. 3: Creating Hull-House and an International Presence, 1889-1900*. Edited by Maree De Angury, Mary Lynn McCree Bryan, and Ellen Skerrett. Urbana: University Of Illinois Press.

Alexander, Lauren Ashley. 2010. "Interview with Clarice Durham." *Oral Histories, Chicago Anti-Apartheid Collection, College Archives & Special Collections, Columbia College Chicago*, April. http://digitalcommons.colum.edu/cadc_caam_oralhistories/10.

"Annie Malone: First African American Millionairess (Educator, Entrepreneur & Philanthropist) -- Courtesy of the Freeman Institute. www.porocollege.com." n.d. www. freemaninstitute.com. https://www.freemaninstitute.com/poro.htm.

Ashbaugh, Carolyn. 2013. *Lucy Parsons: An American Revolutionary*. Chicago: Haymarket Books.

Baldwin, Davarian L. 2007. *Chicago's New Negroes: Modernity, the Great Migration, & Black Urban Life*. Chapel Hill: University of North Carolina Press.

Bay, Mia. 2010. *To Tell the Truth Freely: The Life of Ida B. Wells*. New York: Hill And Wang.

Becker, Xena. n.d. "A Woman's Place in Anarchy: Lucy E. Parsons and the Haymarket Riots – Rare Book and Manuscript Library – U of I Library." *Non Solus* (blog). http://www.library.illinois.edu/rbx/2019/02/28/lucy-e-parsons/.

Bennett Kinnon, Joy. 1997. "Etta Moten Barnett: Still on the Case at 96." *Ebony* 52 (12): 54.

Best, Wallace D. 2005. *Passionately Human, No Less Divine Religion and Culture in Black Chicago, 1915-1952*. Princeton: Princeton University Press.

Bethel New Life Records [Box #1, Folder #2, 6a, 8, 10, 19, 23, 24], Special Collections, Chicago Public Library.

Bethel New Life Records [Box #2, Folder #], Special Collections, Chicago Public Library.

Bethel New Life Records [Box #3, Folder #21], Special Collections, Chicago Public Library.

Blain, Keisha N. 2016. "'Confraternity among All Dark Races': Mittie Maude, Lena Gordon and the Practice of Black (Inter)Nationalism in Chicago, 1932-1942." *Palimpsest* 5 (2): 151–81.

Blair, Cynthia M. 2018. *I've Got to Make My Livin': Black Women's Sex Work in Turn-of-The-Century Chicago*. Chicago; London: The University Of Chicago Press.

Boyd, Herb. 2014. "Global Reporter Era Bell Thompson." New York Amsterdam News: The New Black View. February 6, 2014. https://www.amsterdamnews.com/news/2014/feb/06/global-reporter-era-bell-thompson/?page=2.

Carney Smith, Jessie, ed. 1991. *Notable Black American Women: Book II*. Detroit: Gale Research.
ed. 2006. *Encyclopedia of African American Business*. Vol. 1. Westport: Greenwood Press.

Carney Smith, Jessie . 2013. *Black Firsts: 4,000 Ground-Breaking and Pioneering Historical Events*. Canton: Visible Ink Press.

Chatelain, Marcia. 2015. *South Side Girls: Growing up in the Great Migration*. Durham: Duke University Press.

"Chicago Landmarks - Wendell Phillips High School." n.d. City of Chicago. chicago.gov. https://webapps1.chicago.gov/landmarksweb/web/landmarkdetails.htm?lanId=1399.

Chicago Tribune staff, ed. 1986. "Rachel R. Ridley, Black Civic Leader." *Chicago Tribune*, May 4, 1986. https://www.chicagotribune.com/news/ct-xpm-1986-05-04-8602010158-story.html.

Collins, Marva, and Civia Tamarkin. 1990. *Marva Collins' Way: Returning to Excellence in Education*. New York: Tarcher/Putnam.

Cooper, Michael J. n.d. "Florence B. Price." https://florenceprice.com/biography/.

Corcoran, Michael. 2012. *He Is My Story: The Sanctified Soul of Arizona Dranes*. San Francisco: Tompkins Square Books.

Das, Joanna Dee. 2017. *Katherine Dunham: Dance and the African Diaspora*. New York: Oxford University Press.

DeFreece-Wilson, Eileen. 2010. "Era Bell Thompson: Chicago Renaissance Writer." In *PhD Diss*. Rutgers, The State University of New Jersey.

Dickerson, James. 2002. *Just for a Thrill: Lil Hardin Armstrong, First Lady of Jazz*. New York: Cooper Square Press.

"Dr. Harriett Alleyne Rice." n.d. American Medical Women's Association. Accessed March 24, 2023. http://www.amwa-doc.org/wwibios/dr-harriett-alleyne-rice.

Drachman, Virginia G. 2001. *Sisters in Law: Women Lawyers in Modern American History*. Cambridge: Harvard University Press.

Dunham, Katherine. 1994. *A Touch of Innocence: Memoirs of Childhood*. Chicago: University Of Chicago Press.

Dykema, Dan . n.d. "Florence Beatrice Smith (1887-1953)." Encyclopedia of Arkansas. https://www.encyclopediaofarkansas.net/encyclopedia/entry-detail.aspx?entryID=1742.

Engel, Elizabeth. n.d. "Annie Turnbo Malone ." *SHSMO Historic Missourians*. https://historicmissourians.shsmo.org/annie-turnbo-malone.

Era Bell Thompson Papers, [Box #1-14], Chicago Public Library, Woodson Regional Library, Vivian G. Harsh Research Collection of Afro-American History and Literature.

"Era Bell Thompson." 2012. Read North Dakota. 2012. https://web.archive.org/web/20200922032815/www.readnd.org/thompson-era-bell.html.

"Eudora Binga (Johnson)." 2014. BillionGraves. December 12, 2014. billiongraves.com/grave/Eudora-Johnson-Binga/11905902.

Finley, Larry. 2008. "Introduced Black History to Public Schools—Teacher Showed by Example Need for Higher Education,' Consulted at Chicago State, Governors State." *Chicago Sun-Times*, January 1, 2008.

"Florence Beatrice Price Biography." 2014. Biography.com, A&E Networks Television. April 2, 2014. www.biography.com/people/florence-beatrice-price-21120681.

"Florine Stephens, Obituary." 2012. *Chicago Sun-Times*. December 27, 2012. legacy.suntimes.com/obituaries/chicagosuntimes/obituary.aspx?n=florine-stephens&pid=161976468&fhid=15738.

Foulks-Johnson, Mittie. 1920. "The Twentieth Anniversary of Poro College and Opening of Poro Annex." *The Broad Ax*, December 4, 1920. https://www.mmpe.net/blueridge/docs/BroadAx-1920-12-04.pdf. Archive.

Frisbie, Margery. 2002. *An Alley in Chicago: The Life and Legacy of Monsignor John Egan*. New York: Sheed & Ward.

Gardner, Hugh. 1950. "Jesse Binga, Former Banker, Dies Penniless at 85." *The Chicago Defender*, June 24, 1950.

Giddings, Paula J. 2009. *Ida: A Sword Among Lions*. New York: Harper Collins.

Goldstein, Nancy. 2008. *Jackie Ormes: The First African American Woman Cartoonist*. Ann Arbor: University Of Michigan Press.

Goodloe, Trevor. 2008. "Jesse Binga (1865-1950)." Black Past. March 23, 2008. http://www.blackpast.org/african-american-history/binga-jesse-1865-1950.

Grossman, Ron. 2013. "When Policy Kings Ruled ." www.chicagotribune.com. Tribune Publishing. March 10, 2013. http://www.chicagotribune.com/news/ct-per-flash-policy-kings-0303-20130310-story.html.

Hardison, Ayesha K. 2014. *Writing Through Jane Crow*. Charlottesville: University of Virginia Press.

Hast, Adele, and Rima Lunin Schultz. 2001. *Women Building Chicago, 1790-1990*. Bloomington: Indiana University Press.

Henderson, Ashyia N, ed. 2002. *Who's Who Among African Americans*. Detroit, Mi: Gale.

Hendricks, Wanda A. 2013. *Fannie Barrier Williams: Crossing the Borders of Region and Race*. Urbana: University of Illinois Press.

Hill, James. 1992. "West Side Inspiration Nancy Jefferson, 69." *Chicago Tribune*, October 9, 1992. www.chicagotribune.com/news/ct-xpm-1992-10-19-9204040604-story.html.

Hooks, Theresa F. 2008. "'Smokey Comes to Majestic Star for Evening of Stars Preview.'" *The Chicago Defender*, December 2008.

Hunter, Tera W. 2018. "Review | Latina Heroine or Black Radical? The Complicated Story of Lucy Parsons." *The Washington Post*, January 18, 2018. http://www.washingtonpost.com/outlook/latina-heroine-or-black-radical-the-complicated-story-of-lucy-parsons/2018/01/10/2126da90-dead-11e7-8679-a9728984779c_story.html?noredirect=on&utm_term=.49d07f8db6d9.

"Ida Ray Nelson." n.d. African American Registry. aaregistry.org/story/ida-gray-nelson-dentist-born/.

Jackson, Angela. 2017. *A Surprised Queenhood in the New Black Sun: The Life & Legacy of Gwendolyn Brooks*. Boston: Beacon Press.

Jackson, Barbara Garvey. 1977. "Florence Price, Composer." *The Black Perspective in Music* 5 (1): 31–43.

James McGrath Morris. 2015. *Eye on the Struggle: Ethel Payne, the First Lady of the Black Press*. New York: Harper Collins.

Jenkins, Sherman L. 2016. *Ted Strong Jr.: The Untold Story of an Original Harlem Globetrotter and Negro Leagues All-Star*. New York: Rowman & Littlefield.

Johnson Lewis, Jone. 2019. "Lucy Parsons: Radical and Anarchist, Person of Color, IWW Founder." ThoughtCo. Dotdash Meredith. February 27, 2019. https://www.thoughtco.com/lucy-parsons-biography-3530417.

Johnson, John H. , ed. 1986. "Dr. Agnes Lattimer Named Head of Chicago Hospital." *Jet*, February 24, 1986.

Jones, Jacqueline. 2017. *Goddess of Anarchy: The Life and Times of Lucy Parsons, American Radical*. Basic Books.

Jones-Hogu, Barbara. 2014. Barbara Jones-Hogue interviewed at the South Side Community Art Center Interview by Rebecca Zurich and Skyla Hearn. *Never the Same: Conversations about Art Transforming Politics & Community in Chicago & Beyond*. https://never-the-same.org/interviews/barbara-jones-hogu/.

Katz, William Loren. 2012. "Lucy Gonzales Parsons." Zinn Education Project. Zinn Education Project. 2012. http://www.zinnedproject.org/materials/lucy-gonzales-parsons.

Knupfer, Anne Meis. 2006. *The Chicago Black Renaissance and Women's Activism*. Urbana, Ill: University Of Illinois Press ; Chesham.

Krapp, Kristine M. 1999. "Ida Gray." In *Notable Black American Scientists*. London: Gale.

"Lucy Parsons: Woman of Will | Industrial Workers of the World." n.d. Industrial Workers of the World. Women's History Information Project. https://archive.iww.org/history/biography/LucyParsons/1/.

"Madeline Stratton Morris's Biography." n.d. The History Makers. Accessed March 24, 2023. https://www.thehistorymakers.org/biography/madeline-stratton-morris-39.

Manheim, James M. 2018. "Price, Florence B. 1887-1953." Encyclopedia.com. Gale. May 21, 2018. https://www.encyclopedia.com/people/history/historians-miscellaneous-biographies/florence-price.

"Massachusetts Historical Society | Phillis Wheatley." 2021. Masshist.org. 2021. https://www.masshist.org/features/endofslavery/wheatley.

McClain, Leanita. 1986. *A Foot in Each World: Essays and Articles*. Edited by Clarence Page. Chicago: Northwestern University Press.

Megan, Graydon. 2018. "Teacher and Activist Took on Social Justice Causes." *Chicago Tribune*, 2018. www.digitaledition.chicagotribune.com/infinity/article_share.aspx?guid=6bb5cb88-a8d4-4f0f-943e-4a236e1f6af4.

———. 2019. "Agnes Lattimer, Who Became Cook County Hospital Medical Director and Campaigned against Lead Poisoning, Dies." *Chicago Tribune*, March 1, 2019. https://www.chicagotribune.com/news/obituaries/ct-met-agnes-lattimer-obituary-20180228-story.html.

Michaeli, Ethan. 2016. *The Defender: How the Legendary Black Newspaper Changed America: From the Age of the Pullman Porters to the Age of Obama*. Boston: Houghton Mifflin Harcourt.

Moore, Natalie Y. 2016. *The South Side: A Portrait of Chicago and American Segregation.* New York: St. Martin's Press.

"Nostalgia: Destination Freedom Radio Program – Auction Finds." 2012. Myauctionfinds. com. WordPress. August 14, 2012. http://myauctionfinds.com/2012/08/14/ nostalgia-destination-freedom-radio-program.

Platt, Anthony M, and E. Franklin Frazier. (1932) 2001. *The Negro Family in the United States.* Notre Dame: University Of Notre Dame Press.

Quintana, Maria. 2009. "Annie Turnbo Malone (1869-1957) ." Black Past. December 20, 2009. http://www.blackpast.org/african-american-history/annie-turnbo-malone-1869-1957/.

Rashid, Hakim M., and Zakiyyah Muhammad. 1992. "The Sister Clara Muhammad Schools: Pioneers in the Development of Islamic Education in American." *The Journal of Negro Education* 61 (2): 178=85.

Reed, Christopher Robert. 1999. "Beyond Chicago's Black Metropolis: A History of the West Side's First Century, 1837-1940." *Journal of the Illinois State Historical Society (1998-)* 92 (2): 119–49.

———. 2014. *Knock at the Door of Opportunity: Black Migration to Chicago, 1900-1919.* Carbondale: Southern Illinois University Press.

Reese, Linda W. 2013. "Florence Beatrice Smith Price (1887-1953)." Black Past. January 10, 2013. https://www.blackpast.org/african-american-history/ price-florence-beatrice-smith-1887-1953.

"Rice, Harriet Alleyne (1866-1958)." n.d. Digital.janeaddams.ramapo.edu. The Jane Addams Project at Ramapo College of New Jersey. http://digital.janeaddams.ramapo.edu/items/ show/1429.

Rockliff, Mara, and Michele Wood. 2018. *Born to Swing: Lil Hardin Armstrong's Life in Jazz.* Honesdale: Calkins Creek.

Robert O. French Papers [Box 1, Folders 1-16], Vivian G. Harsh Research Collection of Afro-American History and Literature, Chicago Public Library.

Salter, Daren. 2008. "Scottsboro Trials." Encyclopedia of Alabama. February 6, 2008. http:// encyclopediaofalabama.org/article/h-1456.

Schomburg Center for Research in Black Culture, Jean Blackwell Hutson Research and Reference Division, The New York Public Library. "Mary Fitzbutler Waring, M. D." New York Public Library Digital Collections. Accessed April 28, 2023. https://digitalcollections. nypl.org/items/510d47dd-ebf3-a3d9-e040-e00a18064a99

Schroeder Schlabach, Elizabeth. 2012. *Along the Streets of Bronzeville.* Urbana: University of Illinois Press.

Sensei, Seren. 2017. "Hidden Figures: Ida Gray Nelson Rollins." Video. *YouTube.* https://www. youtube.com/watch?v=9dIMjeTBSko.

Smith, Christina M. 2015. "The Shifting Structure of Chicago's Organized Crime Network and the Women It Left Behind." University of Massachusetts, Amherst.

Smith, J Clay. 2000. *Rebels in Law: Voices in History of Black Women Lawyers.* Ann Arbor: University Of Michigan Press.

Spear, Allan H. 2015. *Black Chicago: The Making of a Negro Ghetto, 1890-1920.* Chicago: University Of Chicago Press.

Steele, Bobbie L. 2011. *Woman of Steele: A Personal and Political Journal.* AuthorHouse.

Stokes, Keith. 2014. "A Woman of Valor." www.eyesofglory.com. October 3, 2014. https:// www.eyesofglory.com/a-woman-of-valor.

Taylor, Ula Yvette. 2017. *The Promise of Patriarchy: Women and the Nation of Islam.* Chapel Hill: The University Of North Carolina Press.

The Appeal. 1909. "Eighth Regiment Ladies' Auxiliary.," July 31, 1909. https://www. newspapers.com/clip/8865716/eighth_regiment_ladies_auxiliary_the/.

The Black Panther. 1969. "Breakfast Programs: Free Breakfast for Children to Be Vamped Up.," July 19, 1969.

Trotter, Greg. 2022. "The Forgotten Legacy of Gertrude Snodgrasss, Cofounder of the Chicago Food Depository." *Chicago*, March 23, 2022.

Trout, Carlynn. n.d. "AAUW Annie Turnbo Malone | Columbia (MO) Branch." American Association of University Women. Accessed March 24, 2023. https://columbia-mo.aauw.net/notablewomen/womenfm/annie-malone.

Walker-McWilliams, Marcia. 2016. *Reverend Addie Wyatt: Faith and the Fight for Labor, Gender, and Racial Equality.* Urbana: University of Illinois Press.

Walwyn, Karen. 2021. "Biography." Florence Price. March 31, 2021. https://florenceprice.com/biography/.

Warnes, Kathy. 2022. "Lucy Parsons, 'More Dangerous than a Thousand Rioters.'" Women of Every Complexion and Complexity. 2022. https://www.womenofeverycomplexionandcomplexity.weebly.com/lucy-parsons-more-dangerous-than-a-thousand-rioters.html.

Warren, Christian. 2001. *Brush with Death: A Social History of Lead Poisoning.* Baltimore: Johns Hopkins University Press.

Washington, Sylvia Hood. 2008. "Mrs. Block Beautiful: African American Women and the Birth of the Urban Conservation Movement, Chicago, Illinois, 1917–1954." *Environmental Justice* 1 (1): 13–23. https://doi.org/10.1089/env.2008.0505.

West, E. James. 2022. *A House for the Struggle: The Black Press and the Built Environment in Chicago.* Urbana: University of Illinois Press.

Whitaker, Charles. 1986. "Cook County's Top Doctor: Agnes Lattimer, M.D. Heads One of Nation's Largest Hospitals." *Ebony*, 1986.

White, C. Rae. 2012. "Eudora Johnson Binga (1871-1933) - Find a Grave..." www.findagrave.com. October 12, 2012. https://www.findagrave.com/memorial/98761731/eudora-binga.

ABOUT HAYMARKET BOOKS

Haymarket Books is a radical, independent, nonprofit book publisher based in Chicago. Our mission is to publish books that contribute to struggles for social and economic justice. We strive to make our books a vibrant and organic part of social movements and the education and development of a critical, engaged, and internationalist Left.

We take inspiration and courage from our namesakes, the Haymarket Martyrs, who gave their lives fighting for a better world. Their 1886 struggle for the eight-hour day—which gave us May Day, the international workers' holiday—reminds workers around the world that ordinary people can organize and struggle for their own liberation. These struggles—against oppression, exploitation, environmental devastation, and war—continue today across the globe.

Since our founding in 2001, Haymarket has published more than nine hundred titles. Radically independent, we seek to drive a wedge into the risk-averse world of corporate book publishing. Our authors include Angela Y. Davis, Arundhati Roy, Keeanga-Yamahtta Taylor, Eve Ewing, Aja Monet, Mariame Kaba, Naomi Klein, Rebecca Solnit, Olúfẹ́mi O. Táíwò, Mohammed El-Kurd, José Olivarez, Noam Chomsky, Winona LaDuke, Robyn Maynard, Leanne Betasamosake Simpson, Howard Zinn, Mike Davis, Marc Lamont Hill, Dave Zirin, Astra Taylor, and Amy Goodman, among many other leading writers of our time. We are also the trade publishers of the acclaimed Historical Materialism Book Series.

Haymarket also manages a vibrant community organizing and event space in Chicago, Haymarket House, the popular Haymarket Books Live event series and podcast, and the annual Socialism Conference.